INNOVATIONS

The Comprehensive Infant & Toddler Curriculum

Trainer's Guide

INNOVATIONS

The **Comprehensive**
Infant
&Toddler
CURRICULUM

Trainer's Guide

Linda G. Miller / Kay Albrecht ●

Illustrations: Joan Waites
Photographs: Kay Albrecht, Masami Mizukami, Rene Summers, and CLEO Photography
Cover photograph: © 2000, Artville

Bulk Purchase

Gryphon House books are
available at special
discount when purchased in
bulk. Special editions or
book excerpts also can be
created to specification. For
details, contact the Director
of Sales at the address or
phone number on this page.

Disclaimer

The publisher and the authors cannot be held
responsible for injury, mishap, or damages
incurred during the use of or because of the
information or activities in this book. The authors
recommend appropriate and reasonable
supervision at all times based on the age and
capability of each child.

Table of Contents

Introduction

For Trainers and Directors

Innovations: The Comprehensive Infant Curriculum and *Innovations: The Comprehensive Toddler Curriculum* are books that provide numerous resources for teachers. Teachers first beginning to use *Innovations* will vary widely in their natural abilities, levels of education/training, amount and quality of experience, and commitment to professional development. Because of this, the *Innovations* series has a variety of supports for directors and trainers to provide professional development to teachers.

Four types of professional development activities are provided by *Innovations: The Comprehensive Infant and Toddler Curriculum, Trainer's Guide*.

1. Comprehensive Introduction to the *Innovations* series (approximately 8 hours)—Section I of this book
2. 29 Inservice/Preservice/Workshops on various topics (approximately 1 to 2 hours per topic)—Section II of this book
3. 29 professional development sessions for biweekly/monthly meetings (approximately 30 minutes to 1 hour)—Section II of this book

The fourth type of professional development is independent study with the support of a mentor or trainer. See *Innovations: The Comprehensive Infant Curriculum, A Self-Directed Teacher's Guide* and *Innovations: The Comprehensive Toddler Curriculum, A Self-Directed Teacher's Guide* for complete training activities for individual teachers. These teachers' guides, available separately from Gryphon House, provide over 40 hours of independent study designed to be supported by a mentor or trainer.

We recommend that the different types of training be used in combination with each other. For instance, when a new school is opening, the director or trainer may find it helpful to conduct a comprehensive introduction (Section I), and then support teachers' professional development as they begin to implement the program through in-service workshops (Section II), staff meetings (Section II), or independent study using **Innovations: The Comprehensive Infant Curriculum, A Self-Directed Teacher's Guide** and **Innovations: The Comprehensive Toddler Curriculum, A Self-Directed Teacher's Guide**. For existing schools, the director or trainer may wish to provide professional development through in-service workshops (Section II) combined with staff meetings (Section II) or independent study. When professional development is difficult to provide, a director/trainer may choose to have teachers go through independent study using **Innovations: The Comprehensive Infant Curriculum, A Self-Directed Teacher's Guide** and **Innovations: The Comprehensive Toddler Curriculum, A Self-Directed Teacher's Guide**. If independent study is the primary professional development activity for teachers, directors/trainers will need to support the teachers by providing other types of training through professional associations and local agencies and by providing ongoing support through observations and conferences.

See page 95 in the appendix for the Preparation Checklist. Use this form to assist you in preparing for any training event. All modules contain a Planning Grid, giving an overview of the entire session. The grid includes topic, description, taxonomy/training technique, and materials. The taxonomy section (in italics) indicates the category on Benjamin Bloom's Taxonomy of educational objectives. The levels go from simple to complex (knowledge, comprehension, application, analysis, synthesis, and evaluation). Additionally, you may find it helpful to read through the detailed agenda in Section I, which has some "extra" training hints.

For more information on Bloom's Taxonomy, see the following:

Bloom, B.S. & D.R. Krathwohl. (1956). **Taxonomy of educational objectives: Handbook I: Cognitive domain**. New York: Longmans, Green.

Jonassen, D., W. Hannum, & M. Tessmer. (1989). "Bloom's taxonomy of educational objectives," Chapter 12 of **Handbook of Task Analysis Procedures**. New York: Praeger.

Krathwohl, D.R., B.S. Bloom, & B.B. Masia. (1964). **Taxonomy of educational objectives: Handbook II: Affective domain**. New York: David McKay Co., Inc.

Comprehensive Introduction to

Innovations: The Comprehensive Infant Curriculum

and

Innovations: The Comprehensive Toddler Curriculum

(APPROXIMATELY 8 HOURS)

Preparation for Comprehensive Introduction to **Innovations** Training
       Handouts/Overheads
       Materials Needed
       Detailed Planning Grid
Detailed Agenda

Preparation for Comprehensive Introduction to *Innovations* Training

1. Secure place and calendar date for the event.
2. Order books for teachers.
3. Communicate the training place, time, and topic to participants.
4. Read the appropriate sections (the entire Getting Started chapters) in both the infant and toddler books.*
5. Secure needed materials (see list on page 13).
6. Copy handouts.
7. Copy overhead transparencies. Punch holes in them and place them in a three-ring binder.
8. Arrange for refreshments, lunch, and breaks.
9. Prepare training certificates.
10. Flip through the books and mark the sections with colored adhesive. (This will make it easier to find each section of the books. In addition, as you introduce different sections of the books, the teachers will mark them. Your books will provide a model for them.)

Note: Structurally, the infant and toddler books are the same; the content is different but related. The toddler curriculum has the addition of Construction as another possibility.

Items I need to copy for overhead transparencies and handouts:

Items I need to gather/purchase:

Notes

Handouts/Overheads

Cover Sheet—page 125

Possibilities Plan (Completed)—page 150

One-day Training Agenda —page 141

Arrow Curriculum Graphic—page 100

PIES—page 144

Relationship of Classroom Challenges to Child Development
  Topics—page 155

Ping-ponging—page 145

Concepts Learned in Me and My Body—page 123

Anecdotal Record—Example of Anetria—page 99

Blank Forms, including

  Anecdotal Record—page 98

  Communication Sheet—page 102

  Books Read List—page 101

  Accident/Incident Report—page 97

  Parent Visit Log—page 142

  Possibilities Plan (Blank)—pages 148

Observation/Assessment Instrument (Relating to Self and
  Others)—page 140

Teacher Competencies to Support Connecting with School and
  Teacher—page 164

Teacher Competencies to Support Making Friends—page 165

Materials Needed

Folders for vocabulary/picture file (Each teacher will need 10 folders
  and numerous pictures from magazines, appropriate junk mail, or
  other sources to place in the file folders.)

Overhead projector

Overhead projector colored pens

Transparencies

Blank forms

Colored tabs

Picture file/vocabulary (example)

Prop box (example)

Choke tester

Magazines

Scissors

Chart paper and easel

Colored broad-tip markers

Nametags

Detailed Planning Grid

Note: The planning grid below is followed by a detailed explanation of the day's activities.

Time	Topic	Description	Training Technique/ Taxonomy	Materials
7:45	Registration			
8:00	Welcome	I Need to Know... List	Listing of Needs *Knowledge, Comprehension*	Flip chart and markers
	Overview of the Day		Mini-lecture *Comprehension*	One-day Training Agenda Overhead/Handout (page 141)
	Comprehensive Curriculum Arrow graphic		Mini-lecture *Knowledge, Comprehension*	Arrow Curriculum Graphic Overhead/Handout (page 100)
	Introductions		Independent Activity, Sharing	
9:00	Developmental Tasks		Flip and mark tasks in books. *Application*	***Innovations*** books for infants and toddlers, tabs
	PIES	Physical, Intellectual, Emotional, Social Domains	Mini-lecture *Knowledge, Comprehension*	PIES Overhead/Handout (page 144), Observation/Assessment Instrument (Relating to Self and Others) Overhead (page 140)
9:30-10:00	Observation and Assessment		Independent Activity Flip and mark assessment instruments in books. *Application*	***Innovations*** books for infants and toddlers, tabs
	Correlate to Planning Form		Mini-lecture *Application*	Possibilities Plan (Completed) Overhead/Handout (page 150)

	Anecdotal Record		Independent Activity *Application*	Anecdotal Record—Example of Anetria Overhead/Handout (page 99)
10:00-10:15	Break			
10:15-10:45	Child Development		Independent Activity Flip and mark using tabs. *Application*	***Innovations*** books for infants and toddlers, tabs
		Classroom challenges and corresponding child development topics.	Demonstration on Overhead *Knowledge, Comprehension*	Relationship of Classroom Challenges to Child Development Topics Overhead/Handout (page 155)
10:45-11:00	Interactive Experiences	Routine Times in the Classroom	Independent Activity Graphic Representation of Ideas Flip and mark using tabs. *Application*	Ping-ponging Overhead/Handout (page 145), Routine Times in the Classroom Overhead (page 161)
11:00-11:15	Teaching		Independent Activity Flip and mark books using tabs. *Application*	***Innovations*** books for infants and toddlers, tabs
	Teacher Competencies		Independent Activity Flip and mark books using tabs. *Application*	***Innovations*** books for infants and toddlers, tabs, Teacher Competencies from Infant and Toddler Books Overhead/Handout (pages 164–165)

11:15-11:30	Parent Partnerships		Independent Activity Flip and mark books using tabs. *Application*	*Innovations* books for infants and toddlers, tabs
	Communication Sheet		Practice Practice filling out forms. *Application*	Communication Sheets Overhead/Handout (page xxx)
11:30-12:00	Environments	Discuss creating environments for young children.	Facilitator-led Discussion *Knowledge, Comprehension, Application*	Creating Environments for Young Children Overhead (page 126), Classroom Checklist Handout (page 127)
12:00-1:00	Lunch			
1:00-1:15	Activities and Experiences		Independent Activity Flip and mark pages using tabs. *Application*	Possibilities Plan Overhead/Handout (page 148)
1:15-2:15	Webbing		Practice Flip and mark pages and create webs. *Application, Analysis*	*Innovations* books for infants and toddlers, tabs, transparency sheets, and markers
2:15-2:30	Planning Pages		Independent Activity Flip and mark books using tabs. *Application*	*Innovations* books for infants and toddlers, tabs

Time	Topic		Method	Materials
2:30-3:00	Possibilities		Independent Activity, Facilitator-led Discussion Flip and mark books using tabs. *Comprehension, Application*	***Innovations*** books for infants and toddlers, tabs
3:00-3:30	Concepts Learned, Resources		Independent Activity Flip and mark pages using tabs. *Application*	Concepts Learned in Me and My Body Overhead/Handouts (page 123), prop box (example), choke tester, picture file/vocabulary folders (example, magazines, file folders), index cards
3:30-3:45	Break			
3:45-4:45	Forms and Other Means of Communication with Parents		Multiple Scribes *Application, Analysis, Synthesis*	(See list on page 27)
4:45-5:00	Summary, Closing, and Evaluation	Review I Need to Know list	Reflection, Questions, and Answers *Synthesis, Evaluation*	Choose a Workshop Evaluation from appendix
	Follow-up		Mentor/trainer looks for evidence of resources in the classroom (Vocabulary/Picture File, Prop Boxes, Temperament Chart, Possibilities Plans, Books Read Lists, and Concepts Learned) *Application, Analysis*	

● Use *Innovations*: BIG IDEA in summary.

Innovations: BIG IDEAS

▶ Development is integrated across four domains—physical, intellectual, emotional, and social.

▶ Understanding child development leads to understanding behaviors.

▶ Interactions matter!

▶ Routines ARE interactions.

▶ Begin everything with observation.

▶ Test all materials for safety before using them in the classroom.

▶ Parents are their child's first and most important teachers.

▶ Create partnerships with parents.

▶ Environments teach.

▶ Webbing opens up possibilities.

▶ Planning is preparation for interactions.

▶ Children are always constructing their own knowledge and learning through their experiences.

▶ Teachers need numerous resources and can make many of them.

Detailed Agenda

7:45-8:00 REGISTRATION

Coffee and refreshments
Registration
Nametags

8:00-8:30 WELCOME AND OVERVIEW

Welcome
Books at tables
Water provided on tables or at station in back of room

Water will help the participants remain alert. Also, make sure the room temperature is set low enough to compensate for the body heat of the participants. Keep in mind that a room that is comfortable before anyone arrives may be uncomfortable when filled with people.

Goal of Training: To prepare the teachers to use *Innovations* to teach
 infants and toddlers.
Learning Outcome: Teachers will be able to implement *Innovations*.

I Need to Know . . . List
Begin by asking the teachers if they have specific questions and list these on a flip chart titled "I Need to Know . . ." Common concerns include biting, tantrums, critical parents, assessment, and toilet training. List all that are voiced, and try to address concerns as they naturally occur during training throughout the day. As the last part of training in the afternoon, read through the list and summarize how the topics were addressed. Check off each one. If any topics were not addressed, discuss them at that time.

Overhead One-day Training Agenda (page 141)
 Handout One-day Training Agenda (page 141)

Overhead Arrow Curriculum Graphic (page 100)
 Handout Arrow Curriculum Graphic (page 100)

Discuss how *Innovations* is different from most curricula. While most curriculum books are very narrow in scope, including only activities, *Innovations* is comprehensive—it includes all the different elements shown in the arrow. All of the elements in the arrow are essential and will be a part of the training.

8:30-8:50 INTRODUCTIONS

If you are training a relatively small group, the individuals can speak to the entire group. If you are training a large group, ask the individuals to speak to the teachers at their own table. Ask the teachers to include in their introductions whether they teach infants or toddlers, where they teach, how long they have taught, and why they chose to teach infants or toddlers. Thank all the teachers, and recognize those with the longest and shortest amount of time teaching. You may choose other icebreakers from the appendix (page 130-132).

8:50-9:00 SHARING

Ask the teachers to share with their neighbor about someone important to them. Welcome photographs if people have them. You'll probably have new parents and grandparents with lots of pictures to share! After a brief time of sharing, talk about the importance of attachment, both for infants and toddlers as well as for adults. By sharing information about someone who is important to them, teachers have attached emotional significance to the day. Because of this, they will remember more from the training experience. (Children and adults thrive in an environment that is warm and secure.)

9:00-9:30 DEVELOPMENTAL TASKS

 Flip to and tab developmental tasks sections in the books.

Developmental tasks are a new way to conceptualize how children grow and learn. They offer teachers a way to view the development of children in large, interrelated tasks instead of in piecemeal, bit-by-bit steps. The six developmental tasks contained in each **Innovations** curriculum are roughly sequential and allow teachers to see small observable steps (for example, in Separating from Parents S2a, infants are "startled by new sounds, smells, and people") within the context of the major developmental task (in this case, separating from parents).

Overhead PIES (page 144)
 Handout PIES (page 144)

Often we think of child development in the domains of Physical Development, Intellectual Development, Emotional Development, and Social Development. Some teachers find it helpful to think of PIES to remember the domains.

Give examples of each type of development:

> ⯈ Physical—"uses motor movements to enhance sensory exploration of the environment"
> ⯈ Intellectual—"shows understanding of simple phrases by responding or reaction"
> ⯈ Emotional—"calms self with transitional objects"
> ⯈ Social—"seeks interaction with familiar people"

FORMS Overhead Observation/Assessment (Relating to Self and Others) (page 140)

Point to the different subtasks on the overhead and ask the teachers to decide whether the subtask is physical, intellectual, emotional, or social. If there is disagreement, don't be concerned. Remind the teachers that the younger the child, the more overlap they'll see among the different domains.

9:30–10:00 OBSERVATION AND ASSESSMENT

DO THIS Flip to and tab the observation and assessment instruments in the books.

Before teachers know what experiences are appropriate for infants and toddlers, they must first observe and assess. This is not testing! It is sensitively determining what young children need. Teachers should plan to mark the observation and assessment instrument as children are engaged in things they naturally do in the classroom. They should keep the observation and assessment instruments for each child on separate clipboards, so they will be convenient to use during the day. Remind them always to date the developmental subtask when they observe it.

FORMS Overhead Possibilities Plan (Completed) (page 150)
Handout Possibilities Plan (Completed)(page 150)

Teachers' observations and assessments are only supportive of a child's learning experiences if they use them to determine appropriate actions for themselves and the child and also to discern a child's developmental needs over time. By including where children are developmentally on the Possibilities Plan, teachers are better able to plan for and address individual needs.

FORMS Overhead Anecdotal Record—Example of Anetria (page 99)
Handout Anecdotal Record—Example of Anetria (page 99)

Read the anecdotal record example of Anetria. Then give the teachers an opportunity to mark the Observation/Assessment Instrument (Relating to Self and Others) (page 140). When they have finished, put the observation and assessment instrument for the developmental task Relating to Self and Others on the overhead again. Ask the teachers to tell you what they marked as a result of the anecdotal record. Discuss briefly.

10:00-10:15   BREAK

10:15-10:45   CHILD DEVELOPMENT

DO THIS Flip to and tab the child development sections in the books.

Often issues that are identified as behavior issues are actually child development issues. For example, look at the issues on the "I Need to Know…" list from earlier in the morning. Point out the items that relate to child development.

Overhead Relationship of Classroom Challenges to Child Development Topics
    (page 155)
FORMS Handout Relationship of Classroom Challenges to Child Development Topics
    (page 155)

All of the topics shown on the overhead as child development issues can be found in the indexes of the books. Use **Innovations** as a handbook (by looking up things in the index, table of contents, or even on the possibilities planning pages) to find out about topics that are important for you in the classroom. Ask the teachers to research a topic that is important to them using their **Innovations** books.

10:45-11:00   INTERACTIVE EXPERIENCES

DO THIS Flip to and tab the interactive experiences in the books.

Interactions between children and their teachers, other children, and parents are a crucial part of each day. In fact, the size of a child's vocabulary is directly influenced by how much the child's teacher talks with her or him. Ira Gordon, in **Baby Learning through Baby Play,** calls the interactions between infant or toddler and the teacher "ping-ponging" because the teacher observes the young child, comments or reacts in some way, and then the young child does the same. Then the teacher reacts, and so on.

FORMS Overhead Ping-ponging (page 145)
Handout Ping-ponging (page 145)

Notice that the teacher is not "doing something" to the child or trying to get the child to do a particular thing. Instead, the interaction is a gentle interchange between adult and child as two equals. The adult modifies and adjusts her or his response based on the observation of the child's response.

FORMS Overhead Routine Times in the Classroom (page 161)

Because so much of a teacher's day is involved with the routine care of children, sometimes it seems impossible to "teach." How can teachers support quality interactions when they are diapering, napping, and feeding? Interactions naturally occur during routine times. Therefore, teachers can make the games, lullabies, songs, and fingerplays a natural part of care routines. Show on the overhead how different interactions match with different routine times. Ask the teachers to think of others.

11:00-11:15   TEACHING

DO THIS Flip to and tab the teaching sections in the books.

The **Innovations** in Teaching sections provide information for teachers from a teacher's perspective. Often a topic that is provided as a postcard for parents is included in the **Innovations** in Teaching section for teachers. Topics such as infant and toddler temperament, primary teaching, nutrition, and stimulating emotional development are all topics found in **Innovations** in Teaching.

Overhead Teacher Competencies to Support Connecting with School and
    Teacher (page 164)
FORMS Handout Teacher Competencies to Support Connecting with School and
    Teacher (page 164)

Overhead Teacher Competencies to Support Making Friends (page 165)
FORMS Handout Teacher Competencies to Support Making Friends (page 165)

The teacher competencies found in each **Innovations** in Teaching section may be used in a number of different ways. Teachers may use them with peer teachers to get the perspective of someone else in the classroom; supervisors may use them to provide feedback for the classroom teacher; and teachers may use them as self-evaluations to determine the areas on which they want to focus for professional development. Give the teachers a few minutes to mark either the infant or toddler set of teacher competencies in their handouts, so they can see their areas of strengths and areas to target.

11:15-11:30   PARENT PARTNERSHIPS

DO THIS ▶ Flip to and tab the parent partnerships sections in the books.

Parents are their child's first and most important teachers. **Innovations** provides many different ways the classroom teacher can support parents in this primary role.

FORMS ▶ Overhead Communication Sheet (page 102)

The communication sheet supports parents as being knowledgeable about their child. The sheet also lets parents know what kind of day their child has had. Teachers should always write neatly and fill out the form completely.

FORMS ▶ Handout Communication Sheet (page 102)

Provide the teachers with copies of the Communication Sheet and ask them to complete the form for a child for one day. When they are finished, ask them to exchange forms and give feedback.

11:30-12:00   ENVIRONMENTS

DO THIS ▶ Flip to and tab the **Innovations** in Environments sections in the books.

FORMS ▶ Overhead Creating Environments for Young Children (page 126)
Handout Classroom Checklist (page 127)

Discuss the overhead—Creating Environments for Young Children. Then ask the teachers to complete the Classroom Checklist handout. Discuss the results. Environments actually teach children through their active exploration.

12:00-1:00   LUNCH

Because it is difficult for the teachers to leave to get lunch and then return in one hour, if at all possible, provide lunch or plan for a brown bag lunch and provide drinks. In this way, you can begin at 1:00 and also make everyone happy because you have provided part or all of lunch. Try to avoid large or "heavy" meals. These can challenge both you and the teachers to have enough energy and alertness for the afternoon activities.

Overhead Possibilities Plan (page 148)
Handout Possibilities Plan (page 148)

Discuss the difference between activities and experiences in the **Innovations** books and centers/areas that we normally think of with preschool children (see pages 24-28 in the infant book and pages 25-30 in the toddler book). Also talk about how varied the activities are. Show the teachers the Possibilities Plan handout/overhead. (They will have an opportunity to practice lesson planning later in the day.) Explain that the list of possibilities for both the infant and toddler lesson plans are the same except for construction, which is only for toddlers. Activities and experiences enable the teachers to prepare the environment with appropriate materials and provide quality interactions with individual infants and toddlers.

1:15-2:15   WEBBING

Webbing is a curriculum development technique that allows teachers to view curriculum as being emergent in nature. A web can show teachers some of the many ways that a Possibility Plan can go. Webs are included for all 12 Possibilities Plans presented in both the infant and the toddler books.

Flip and tab web pages in the **Innovations** books.

Next give each group a blank transparency sheet and markers. Ask the groups to create their own webs using topics found in the **Innovations** books or using their own topics. After the groups have completed their webs, ask the group leaders to present the webs using the overhead projector.

2:15-2:30   PLANNING PAGES

Flip and tab the planning pages in the **Innovations** books.

Each Possibility Plan (12 in each book) has the page numbers to show where to find the activities. For example, ask the teachers to look on pages 190-191 (Big and Little) in the infant book or pages 192-193 (Fruits and Vegetables) in the toddler book. Give the teachers time to practice going from the activity titles on the planning pages to the actual activities on the pages referenced.

2:30-3:00 POSSIBILITIES

DO THIS Flip and tab the possibilities sections in the *Innovations* books.

Explanations of the different types of possibilities are on pages 25-28 in the infant book and pages 25-30 in the toddler book. Again, emphasize the differences in the possibilities and traditional centers or areas. Discuss each of the possibilities and give an example from both the infant book and the toddler book.

Possibilities
>   Dramatic
>   Sensory/Art
>   Curiosity
>   Construction (in toddler book only)
>   Literacy
>   Music
>   Outdoor
>   Projects
>   Parent Participation (These are ideas in addition to those included in Parent Partnerships.)

3:00-3:30 CONCEPTS LEARNED AND RESOURCES

 FORMS Overhead Concepts Learned in Me and My Body (page 123)
Handout Concepts Learned in Me and My Body (page 123)

Concepts Learned lists show parents what their children are doing during the day. All the Concepts Learned lists are collected and included in the appendix of each book (pages 452-463 in the infant book and pages 558-569 in the toddler book). This is a way for teachers to provide documentation of what children have learned. The teachers use the handout, writing in children's names and dates next to the concept learned. Using overhead markers, add the children's names, dates, and additional concepts to the overhead of Concepts Learned in Me and My Body from the toddler book.

Resources are included at the end of each Possibilities Plan in both the infant and toddler *Innovations* books. Resources include all of the following:
>   Prop Boxes
>   Picture File/Vocabulary
>   Books
>   Rhymes/Fingerplays
>   Music/Songs
>   Toys and Materials (purchased and gathered)

Ask the teachers to turn to the Resources section in either the infant or the toddler book. Briefly discuss each of the types of resources. Show an example of a prop box that you have created. Brainstorm a plan for obtaining boxes to store items. (Copypaper boxes work well, and often parents are able to get these from their workplaces. Clear plastic containers also work well.) Stress the importance of attaching a list of all the materials included in the prop box to the lid. Also, as with all items brought into the classroom, teachers should carefully inspect all items for safety. Illustrate this by testing items in the prop box using a choke tester. Show the teachers the picture file/vocabulary folders you have created. Give the teachers time to begin their own files by cutting out pictures from magazines and writing category names on the file folders. Also, show the index cards on which you have written vocabulary words (simple words printed in lower case letters). Provide index cards so the teachers can do the same.

3:30-3:45   BREAK

(Some teachers may choose to continue working on their picture files/vocabulary.)

3:45-4:45   FORMS AND OTHER MEANS OF
                 COMMUNICATION WITH PARENTS

 Overhead   Forms (see below)

Forms can assist teachers as they document events in the classroom, communicate with parents, and plan for quality experiences for children. Show examples of the forms listed below on the overhead projector. Ask the teachers if they have any questions concerning any of the following forms.

> Anecdotal Record (page 98)
>
> Communication Sheet (page 102)
>
> Books Read List (page 101)
>
> Accident/Incident Report (page 97)
>
> Parent Visit Log (page 142)
>
> Complete Observation/Assessment, Birth to 18 Months (page 105)
>
> Complete Observation/Assessment, 18 to 36 Months (page 114)
>
> Conference Summary Form (page 124)
>
> Portfolio Planning Form (page 147)

Handout Workshop Evaluation (pages 178-179)

Close the workshop by going over the "I Need to Know . . ." list from the beginning of the day. Answer any questions that have not already been answered. Hand out workshop evaluations. While the teachers are filling out the evaluations, draw for door prizes. Show the teachers evidence of the training they have received (for example, the webs or picture files they created) and explain to them that you (or someone else) will visit classrooms to observe the results of this training.

Follow-up: Director/Mentor/Trainer observes to find evidence of resources in the classroom:

> Vocabulary/Picture File
> Prop Boxes
> Temperament Charts
> Possibilities Plans
> Books Read Lists
> Concepts Learned

Inservice/Preservice/ Workshops on Various Topics

(approximately 1 to 2 hours per topic)

or

Staff Meetings— Biweekly/Monthly

(approximately 30 minutes to 1 hour)

Topics

Module 1: Understanding Child Development Theory: Principles of Development/Physical Development

Module 2: Understanding Child Development Theory: Attachment

Module 3: Understanding Child Development Theory: Temperament

Module 4: Understanding Child Development Theory: Play

Module 5: Understanding Child Development Theory: Brain Development and Intellectual Development

Module 6: Understanding Child Development Theory: Language Development and Literacy

Module 7: Understanding Child Development Theory: Social Development and Social Problem-solving

Module 8: Developmental Tasks

Module 9: Observation and Assessment

Module 10: Interactive Experiences

Module 11: Parent Partnerships

Module 12: Curriculum Planning Process

Module 13: Environments

Module 14: Dramatic Possibilities

Module 15: Sensory/Art Possibilities

Module 16: Curiosity Possibilities

Module 17: Construction Possibilities (for Toddlers)

Module 18: Music/Movement Possibilities

Module 19: Literacy Possibilities

Module 20: Outdoor Possibilities

Module 21: Projects

Module 22: Prop Boxes

Module 23: Picture Files/Vocabulary

Module 24: Guidance and Discipline

Module 25: Biting

Module 26: Aggression

Module 27: Social Problem-solving

Module 28: Toileting

Module 29: Portfolios

Note: Trainer/director will need to adjust times and number of activities accordingly. Fill in approximate times on the training grid as part of preparation for each individual workshop.

Understanding Child Development Theory: Principles of Development/Physical Development

- Complete Preparation Checklist in appendix (page 95).

- Read appropriate sections of books, including pages 34-35 in the infant book and pages 40-42 in the toddler book.

READ THIS

Time	Topic	Description	Taxonomy/ Training Technique	Materials
	Introduction and Housekeeping			
	Getting Better Acquainted	Choose ice breaker from appendix.	Ice Breaker	Materials given in appendix
	Understanding Underlying Child Development Principles		Poll Teachers Needs Assessment: "What I Need to Know…" Chart *Comprehension*	Chart paper, markers
	Principle 1: Development follows a universal and predictable sequence.		Create Time Line Graphic Representation of Information—Time Line Activity *Knowledge*	Paper, markers
	Principle 2: Each child has an individual pattern and timing of growth.		Poll Teachers, Facilitator-led Discussion Discovering Individual Patterns of Growth and Development *Knowledge, Comprehension*	
	Age is a poor predictor of developmental stage.		Summary Concerned Parent Simulation *Synthesis*	Paper, pens/pencils

	Principle 3: Development proceeds from the simple to complex and from general to specific.		Math Questions Worksheet *Comprehension*	
	Understand the connections between child development theory and practice and children's behavior.		Ask teachers to list behaviors that present problems in their classrooms. *Application*	
	Explore the underlying child development issues that correlate with the behavior.		Poll Teachers Behavior/Development Activity *Application*	Chart paper; 3 x 5 index cards, markers, pens/pencils
	Infant and toddler behavior often has a developmental explanation.		Summary, Handout completion *Synthesis*	Relationship of Classroom Challenges to Child Development Topics Overhead/Handout (page 155)
	Physical Development: Using physical development to illustrate the three principles.		Using Case Studies to Understand Development *Comprehension*	Anecdotal Record (Blank) (page 98), **Innovations** infant and toddler books
	BIG IDEA: Doing a developmental skill first (or last) is not related to potential or future outcomes.		Summary, Predictions *Synthesis*	
	Apply three principles.		Facilitator-led Discussion *Application*	

	Summarize session with BIG IDEAS.		Summary Individual and Small Group Activity *Synthesis*	Relationship of Classroom Challenges to Child Development Topics Overhead/Handout (page 155)
	Innovations: BIG IDEAS "What I Need to Know..."	Summary and Evaluation	Reflection, Questions, and Answers "What I Need to Know..." Chart, Summary *Synthesis, Evaluation*	Chart paper, markers, evaluations (choose one from appendix)

Needs Assessment—"What I Need to Know…" Chart

Introduce the topic and make a "What I Need to Know…" chart. Ask for input from the teachers. Use the chart as you discuss topics throughout the workshop. Check off items as they are discussed.

Graphic Representation of Information—Time Line Activity

Divide the teachers into groups of three. Ask the groups to identify major childhood milestones. Use long horizontal paper to illustrate life events, noting when they occurred. Suggest a few for everyone to complete (high school graduation, marriage, first child, and so on).

Discovering Individual Patterns of Growth and Development

To foster teachers' understanding that children's ages and stages can be similar or different, help them discover their own developmental uniquenesses. Ask participants to line up on a continuum in response to the following: Age of obtaining driver's license, from youngest to oldest; age at graduation from high school, from youngest to oldest; age at time of marriage, from youngest to oldest; age at time of first child's birth. Complete this activity by discussing examples of the individual patterns of timing and growth that the group exhibited. Some may have gotten driver's licenses at 15, others at 16, others at 25, and so on, illustrating the individual nature and timing of life experiences. Apply this to children's unique patterns and timing of growth and development.

Concerned Parent Simulation

Plan what to say to a parent who is concerned that her or his son (14 months) is not yet walking . Share the plans in small groups.

Math Questions Worksheet

Create a worksheet with math questions of increasing complexity. Ask the teachers to complete the problems in groups. Discuss how math skills develop from simple to complex. Then discuss how children's development proceeds from simple to complex and from general to specific.

Behavior/Development Activity

Ask the teachers to identify some behavioral "problems" that they have in their classrooms. Write one problem on each 3 x 5 index card. Ask each teacher to draw a card from the stack and identify the developmental issue related to the behavior. Make a grid on a piece of chart paper and list the behaviors on one side and the developmental issue on the other.

Using Case Studies to Understand Development

Ask the teachers to read their case studies (anecdotal records). Then divide them into small groups and ask them to identify major physical milestones using checklists from the books. Chart when milestones are accomplished to show differences across case studies.

 ### Relationship of Classroom Challenges to Child Development Topics Handout

Ask the teachers to complete the handout and discuss it in groups. If time is short, use the handout as a follow-up activity.

Predictions

Give a description of a child and ask the teachers to predict his or her future. Discuss why or why not predictions are reasonable.

"What I Need to Know..." Chart Summary

Address any topics not already covered on the chart. Check off points as they are addressed.

● Use **Innovations**: BIG IDEAS in summary.

> ## Innovations: BIG IDEAS
>
> ▶ Infant and toddler behavior often has a developmental explanation.
>
> ▶ Age is a poor predictor of developmental stage.
>
> ▶ Performing a developmental skill first (or last) is not related to potential or future outcomes.

Understanding Child Development Theory: Attachment

● Complete Preparation Checklist in appendix (page 95).

● Read appropriate sections of books, including pages 98-100 and 238-240 in the infant book and pages 42-43 in the toddler book.

Time	Topic	Description	Training Technique/ Taxonomy	Materials
	Introduction and Housekeeping			
	Getting Better Acquainted	Choose ice breaker from appendix.	Ice Breaker Poll Teachers	Materials given in appendix
	Understanding Underlying Child Development Principles		Needs Assessment: "What I need to Know…" chart *Comprehension*	Chart paper, markers
	Stage 1 (Indiscriminate Attachment) is where there is less difference in the way babies respond to adults.		Facilitator-led Discussion Discuss examples of indiscriminate attachment. *Comprehension, Application*	
	Stage 2 (Discriminate Attachment) occurs when babies show a definite preference for interaction and comfort from mother, father, or other frequent caregiver.		Facilitator-led Discussion Discuss examples of discriminate attachment. *Comprehension, Application*	

Stage 3 (Separation Anxiety) is where babies show a definite preference for mothers, fathers, and most significant caregivers and resist care from unfamiliar adults.		Facilitator-led Discussion Discuss examples of separation anxiety. *Comprehension, Application*	
Stage 4 (Stranger Anxiety) is where fear of strangers or unknown persons is present.		Facilitator-led Discussion Discuss examples of stranger anxiety. *Comprehension, Application*	
Behaviors are indicators of a child's stage of attachment.		Individual Activity What Stage Activity *Synthesis, Evaluation*	Index cards, pens/pencils
		Round Robin Attachment Questions *Synthesis, Evaluation*	Cards with behaviors and attachment stages
Innovations: BIG IDEAS "What I Need to Know…"	Summary and Evaluation	Summary, Reflection, Questions, and Answers *Synthesis, Evaluation*	Workshop Evaluations (choose from appendix)

What Stage Activity and *Round Robin Attachment Questions*

Ask the teachers to write three specific behaviors related to attachment on one side of an index card. Then ask them to write the stage of attachment on the back of the card. Ask the teachers to use their cards with each other. They can first read the behavior and then ask another teacher to give the stage of attachment. Allow the teachers enough time to ask/be asked all the behaviors on the cards.

Address any topics not already covered on the chart. Check off points as they are addressed.

● Use *Innovations*: BIG IDEAS in summary.

Innovations: BIG IDEAS

▶ Attachment is a process important to a child's development.

▶ Separation anxiety is an integral part of the attachment process.

▶ Stranger anxiety shows progress in the attachment process.

Understanding Child Development Theory: Temperament

● Complete Preparation Checklist in appendix (page 95).

READ THIS ● Read appropriate sections of books, including pages 37-38 in the infant book and pages 43-45 in the toddler book.

Time	Topic	Description	Training/Technique Taxonomy	Materials
	Introduction and Housekeeping			
	Getting Better Acquainted	Choose ice breaker from appendix.	Ice Breaker	Materials given in appendix
	Understanding Temperament in Young Children		Discussion Discuss the three infant/toddler temperaments. *Knowledge, Comprehension*	
	Innovations: BIG IDEAS "What I Need to Know…"		Infant/Toddler Temperament Chart *Synthesis*	Paper, pen/pencil, Infant/Toddler Temperament Chart Overhead/Handout (page 134)
		Summary and Evaluation	Summary, Reflection, Questions, and Answers *Synthesis, Evaluation*	Workshop Evaluations (choose from appendix)
	Follow-up		Determine temperament of children in the group. *Synthesis, Observation*	Infant/Toddler Temperament Chart Overhead (page 134)

Infant/Toddler Temperament Chart

Using the infant/toddler temperament chart, ask the teachers to select a child in their class and determine the child's personality/temperament type. Share a description of a child or show a brief videotape and ask the teachers what personality/temperament is present.

"What I Need to Know..." Chart Summary

Address any topics not already covered on the chart. Check off points as they are addressed.

● Use *Innovations*: BIG IDEAS in summary.

Innovations: BIG IDEAS

▶ Children are born with personality types (for example, fearful, flexible, feisty).

▶ All children (even happy, flexible ones) need attention from caring adults.

Understanding Child Development Theory: Play

4

- Complete Preparation Checklist in appendix (page 95).

READ THIS ➤ • Read appropriate sections of books, including pages 164-166 in the infant book and pages 124-126 in the toddler book.

Time	Topic	Description	Training Technique/ Taxonomy	Materials
	Introduction and Housekeeping			
	Getting Better Acquainted	Choose ice breaker from appendix.	Ice Breaker	Materials given in appendix
	Understanding Play and Young Children	Children learn through play–through the active exploration of materials.	Discussion Chart Paper Activity *Knowledge, Comprehension*	Chart paper, markers, The Value of Play Overhead/ Handout (page 177)
	Masters of Play	Overview of Piaget, Parten, and Vygotsky	Discussion *Knowledge, Comprehension*	***Innovations*** infant and toddler books, Play Theorist Summary Handout (page 146)
	Piaget Play Theory	Discuss Piaget's ideas.	Discussion *Knowledge, comprehension*	
	Parten Play Theory	Discuss Parten's ideas.	Discussion Teachers complete the Parten Types of Play Chart and discuss in groups. *Knowledge, Comprehension*	Parten Types of Play Chart Overhead/ Handout (page 143)

	Vygotsky Play Theory	Discuss Vygotsky's ideas.	Discussion *Knowledge, Comprehension*	
	Innovations: BIG IDEAS	Summary and Evaluation	Reflection, Questions, and Answers *Synthesis, Evaluation*	Workshop evaluations (choose from appendix)

Chart Paper Activity

Attach pieces of chart paper to the wall and label each with a different possibility (dramatic, sensory/art, curiosity, construction (toddlers only), literacy, music/movement, outdoor, and project). Ask the teachers to write under each possibility what children are learning with each type of activity (for example, music–creative movement, singing, counting). Summarize the charts with the entire group and discuss the Value of Play Handout.

● Use ***Innovations***: BIG IDEAS in summary.

Innovations: **BIG IDEAS**

▶ Children learn through play–through the active exploration of materials.

▶ Children participate in different types of play in different environments.

▶ Observing children at play reveals developmental information.

MODULE 5

Understanding Child Development Theory: Brain Development and Intellectual Development

- Complete Preparation Checklist in appendix (page 95).

READ THIS → ● Read appropriate sections of books, including pages 228-232 in the infant book and pages 284-295 in toddler book.

Time	Topic	Description	Training Technique/ Taxonomy	Materials
	Introduction and Housekeeping			
	Getting Better Acquainted	Choose ice breaker from appendix.	Ice Breaker	Materials given in appendix
	Understanding Brain Growth and Development		Reading Graphic Representation of Ideas—Brain Growth Activity *Comprehension*	Markers, colored pencils, chalk, watercolors, paper, and so on (for teachers to draw ideas of how the brain develops)
	Understanding Intellectual Development		Learning Tasks Scavenger Hunt *Application, Analysis*	12 Learning Tasks Handout (page 96)
	Understanding Multiple Intelligences		Large Group Activity, Discussion Teacher Intelligences Activity *Comprehension, Application*	Gardner's Multiple Intelligences Overhead/Handout (page 129)

	Stimulating Language and Cognitive Development—Reading Books	Using children's books to stimulate both language and cognitive skills	Group Activity Using Books to Stimulate Language and Cognitive Skills Activity *Knowledge, Application*	Children's books, flip chart paper, markers
	Innovations: BIG IDEAS	Summary and Evaluation	Reflection, Questions, and Answers *Synthesis, Evaluation*	
	Follow-up		Peer Observations to Assess Language Stimulation Techniques *Application, Analysis*	

Graphic Representation of Ideas—Brain Growth Activity

Ask the teachers to read page 228 in the infant book and pages 284-285 in the toddler book. Then ask them to make a drawing of how the brain grows during infancy and toddlerhood. Post the drawings for all the teachers to view.

Learning Tasks Scavenger Hunt

Send the teachers in teams of two to their classrooms with the list of 12 Learning Tasks Handout (page 96). Ask the teachers to identify one toy or material that fits into each of the 12 tasks. When the teachers return, discuss any tasks that were missing and see if the group can identify an appropriate toy or activity.

Teacher Intelligences Activity

Ask the teachers to pick one or two intelligences from Gardner's Multiple Intelligences Handout (page 129) that they feel are personal strengths. Identify who picked which intelligence by asking the teachers to stand as you call out each type of intelligence. Discuss the differences in the group. Apply the ideas discussed to the children in the teachers' classrooms and discuss what these differences mean to teachers.

Divide the teachers into small groups. Give each group a children's book to read. Ask a teacher in each group to read the book to the rest of the group. Then, ask each group to identify how the book provided stimulation of the language and cognitive domains of development. Ask the groups to list their ideas and then share them with the larger group.

● Use *Innovations*: BIG IDEAS in summary.

Innovations: **BIG IDEAS**

▶ Children and adults learn by using multiple intelligences.

▶ Reading books to children stimulates both language and cognitive skills.

▶ Intelligence is the result of a complex relationship between genes and experiences.

Understanding Child Development Theory: Language Development and Literacy

● Complete Preparation Checklist in appendix (page 95).

● Read appropriate sections of books, including pages 229-234 in the infant book and pages 285-295 in the toddler book.

READ THIS

Time	Topic	Description	Training Technique/ Taxonomy	Materials
	Introduction and Housekeeping			
	Getting Better Acquainted	Choose ice breaker from appendix.	Ice Breaker	Materials given in appendix
	Understanding Language Development		Videotape Viewing Activity *Analysis, Application*	Videotape*, Language Behaviors Checklist Handout (page 136-137), note paper for activities
	Using Language Stimulation Techniques		Pair Activity, Summary, Discussion *Application, Analysis*	Techniques for Stimulating Language Development (with examples) Overhead (page 166)
	Supporting Early Literacy Development		Field Trip in School Activity *Analysis*	Strategies for Supporting Emerging Literacy Handout (page 162-163)
	Innovations: BIG IDEAS	Summary and Evaluation	Reflection, Questions, and Answers *Synthesis, Evaluation*	
	Follow-up		Labels for Classroom Items	

*Ahead of time, videotape infants and toddlers in the classroom as they talk with and to their teachers. The tape should be about five minutes long and have several examples of adults' language and children's language.

Videotape Viewing Activity

Show the videotape. Ask the teachers to use the Language Behaviors Checklist (pages 136-137) to figure out which skills the children in the videotape are demonstrating. Then, ask the teachers to work in pairs to plan an appropriate language stimulation activity for a child in the videotape. Share a few of the activities planned by the teachers. Relate the insight received in this activity to the importance of observation.

Pair Activity

Divide the teachers into pairs. Ask one member of the pair to play while the other practices using the ideas outlined in the Techniques for Stimulating Language Development Overhead (page 166). The teachers switch roles and repeat. After trying out the techniques, encourage the teachers to talk about the experience and what they learned.

Field Trip in School Activity

Send the teachers to their classrooms to determine if they are using appropriate strategies to support early literacy (refer to Strategies for Supporting Emerging Literacy Handout on page 162-163.). Ask several teachers to share one of the ways that they encourage literacy in their classroom and one idea they would like to try.

Labels for Classroom Items

Ask the teachers to create and post picture labels for six to eight classroom items.

● Use *Innovations*: BIG IDEAS in summary.

Innovations: BIG IDEAS

▶ The size of a toddler's vocabulary is a direct result of how much the teacher talks with him or her.

▶ Teachers can support early literacy.

Understanding Child Development Theory: Social Development and Social Problem-solving

● Complete Preparation Checklist in appendix (page 95).

● Read appropriate sections of books, including pages 164-166, 168, 180-181 in the infant book and pages 285-295 in the toddler book.

Time	Topic	Description	Training Technique/ Taxonomy	Materials
	Introduction and Housekeeping			
	Getting Better Acquainted	Choose ice breaker from appendix.	Ice Breaker	Materials given in appendix
	Understanding Social Development	Lecture	Provide an overview of each play theorist including Piaget, Parten, and Vygotsky, briefly summarizing each one. *Knowledge*	Play Theorist Summary Overhead (page 146)
	Understanding Social Problem-solving		Small Groups Conflicts/Social Problem-solving Activity *Analysis*	
	Developmental Stages of Biting		Biting Quiz *Application, Analysis*	Case Studies of Biters (from Problem-solving Activity)
	Handling Biting in the Classroom		Reading, Group Discussion Problem/Solution Activity *Comprehension, Application*	

	Talking with Parents about Biting		Biting Role Play *Comprehension, Application*	Postcards on biting from infant and toddler books
	Innovations: BIG IDEAS	Summary and Evaluation	Reflection, Questions, and Answers *Synthesis, Evaluation*	

Conflicts/Social Problem-solving Activity

Ask the groups to select a recorder to write down the problem as it is described. Then instruct the groups to identify conflicts that arise in the classroom. Then, ask them to select an appropriate social problem-solving strategy for each identified conflict. Continue the discussion by talking about how to teach children the skills they need to use with each strategy.

Biting Quiz

Describe a biting incident identified in the small groups and ask the teachers to identify which stage of biting the child is in.

Problem/Solution Activity

Identify a child who is having problems with aggression or biting. Ask the teacher to share a little about the situations that are causing problems and the strategies that she or he is using to address the problems. Identify which ones are working and which ones aren't. Then ask the teachers to read pages 174-176 in the infant book and pages 136-139 in the toddler book. Finally, ask the teachers to identify which techniques might work for the child who was used as an example.

Biting Role Play

Role-play how to discuss a biting incident with the parent of the child who did the biting and the parent of the child who was bitten. After the role play, ask the teachers how they might use the postcards in the infant and the toddler books that address biting with parents to help them understand developmental biting.

● Use ***Innovations***: BIG IDEAS in summary.

Innovations: BIG IDEAS

▶ Conflicts/problems are a common outgrowth of play.

▶ Conflicts are an opportunity to teach social problem-solving.

▶ Children bite for different reasons at different stages in their development.

Developmental Tasks

● Complete Preparation Checklist in appendix (page 95).

● Read appropriate sections of books, including pages 18, 31-33, 95-97, 161-163, 225-227, 299-300, 365-367 in the infant book and pages 18, 37-39, 121-123, 215-218, 281-283 367-369, 453-455 in the toddler book.

Time	Topic	Description	Training Technique/ Taxonomy	Materials
	Introduction and Housekeeping			
	Getting Better Acquainted	Choose ice breaker from appendix.	Ice Breaker	Materials given in appendix
	Understanding Developmental Tasks	Developmental tasks are a new way to conceptualize how children grow and learn.	Locate developmental tasks in chapters 2-7 in both the infant book and the toddler book	**Innovations** infant and toddler books
	Developmental Tasks for Infants	Roughly sequential	Discussion *Comprehension*	Infant Developmental Tasks Overhead (page 133)
	Developmental Tasks for Toddlers		Discussion *Comprehension*	Toddler Developmental Tasks Overhead (page 167)
	Developmental Domains	Roughly Sequential	Audience Participation *Analysis*	PIES Overhead/Handout (page 144)
	Relationship of Developmental Tasks to Developmental Domains	Ask the teachers to identify in which developmental domains the subtasks are.	Audience Participation *Analysis*	Observation/ Assessment Instrument Overhead (Relating to Self and Others) (page 140)

Overlap of Domains	When there is disagreement on domains, remind teachers that the younger the child, the more overlap there will be.		
Using Tasks to Discuss Development with Parents	Developmental tasks can help parents see development as a process.	Development Role Play *Application*	
Innovations: BIG IDEAS	Summary and Evaluation	Reflection, Questions, and Answers *Synthesis, Evaluation*	Workshop Evaluations (choose from appendix)

Development Role Play

Ask the teachers to role-play using a particular task to discuss development with parents.

● Use ***Innovations***: BIG IDEAS in summary.

Innovations: **BIG IDEAS**

▶ The younger the child, the more we see overlap in the domains of physical, intellectual, emotional, and social development.

▶ Developmental tasks are a new way to conceptualize how children grow and learn.

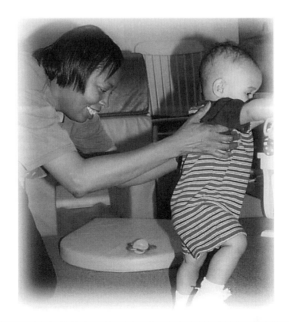

Observation and Assessment

- Complete Preparation Checklist in appendix (page xxx).

- Read appropriate sections of books, including pages 435-440 in the infant book and pages 542-547 in the toddler book.

Time	Topic	Description	Training Technique/ Taxonomy	Materials
	Introduction and Housekeeping			
	Getting Better Acquainted	Choose ice breaker from appendix.	Ice Breaker	Materials given in appendix
	Understanding Observation and Assessment	Observe and assess first before selecting appropriate experiences.	Review Teachers can familiarize themselves with the Combined Infant and Toddler Observation/ Assessment Instrument. *Comprehension*	Copies of Combined Infant and Toddler Observation/ Assessment Instrument (page 183) on individual clipboards
	Relationship of Observation and Assessment to Planning		Discussion *Analysis*	Possibilities Plan (Completed) Overhead (page 150)
	Relationship of Anecdotal Records to Complete Observation and Assessment Instruments	Mark assessment using anecdotal record.	Simulation, Discussion of Results *Analysis*	Anecdotal Record— Example of Anetria Handout (page 99), Observation/ Assessment Instrument (Relating to Self and Others) Handout (page 140)

Observation and Assessment in the Classroom	View videotape and mark assessment instrument.	Simulation, Discussion of Results	Videotape of children in the classroom, copies of Complete Observation/ Assessment Instruments, colored pencils or markers
Innovations: BIG IDEAS	Summary and Evaluation	Analysis Reflection, Questions, and Answers *Synthesis, Evaluation*	Workshop Evaluations (choose from appendix), Anecdotal Records (Blank) (page 98)
Follow-up		Teachers complete three Anecdotal Records.	

● Use *Innovations*: BIG IDEAS in summary.

Innovations: BIG IDEAS

▶ Teachers observe and assess so that they understand what experiences are appropriate.

Interactive Experiences

● Complete Preparation Checklist in appendix (page 95).

● Read appropriate sections of books, including pages 22, 35-36, 101, 166-167, 233-234, 307-308, 369-370, 446 in the infant book and pages 22-23, 45-46, 127-128, 221, 294-295, 373, 457-458 in the toddler book.

Time	Topic	Description	Training Technique/ Taxonomy	Materials
	Introduction and Housekeeping			
	Getting Better Acquainted	Choose ice breaker from appendix.	Ice Breaker	Materials given in appendix
	Understanding Interactive Experiences		Flip and Mark Flip through books to see the Innovations in Interactive Experiences (chapters 2-6). *Comprehension*	***Innovations*** infant and toddler books, tabs
			Individual Activity Interactive Experiences Activity *Application*	Interactive Experiences Checklist Handout (page 135)
	Problems with Application		Discussion, Brainstorm Ask the teachers which items are difficult to apply. Then brainstorm strategies to help apply items on the list. *Application*	Interactive Experiences Checklist Overhead (page 135), markers

| Interactions as Ping-ponging | Ping-ponging shows mutual respect between teacher and child. | Discussion

Comprehension | Ping-ponging Overhead (page 145) |
| The Relationship between Interactive Experiences and Routines | Teachers use routine times for interactions with children. | Questioning

Ask teachers how they can plan for interactions during the routine times.

Application | Routine Times in the Classroom Overhead/Handout (page 161) |
| ***Innovations***: BIG IDEAS | Summary and Evaluation | Reflection, Questions, and Answers

Synthesis, Evaluation | Workshop Evaluations (choose from appendix) |

Interactive Experiences Activity

Ask the teachers to apply interactive experiences to the classroom by writing an example of what they can do next to each item on the list.

● Use ***Innovations***: BIG IDEAS in summary.

Innovations: **BIG IDEAS**

▶ Use routine times to interact with children.

▶ Ping-ponging shows mutual respect between teacher and child.

Parent Partnerships

● Complete Preparation Checklist in appendix (page 95).

● Read appropriate sections of books, including *Innovations* in Parent Partnerships on pages 47-55, 108-118, 177-186, 244-257, 319-325, and 383-386 in the infant book and pages 58-67, 142-157, 227-230, 308-319, 391-402, and 474-484 in the toddler book. Parent Participation Possibilities are included for all 12 Possibilities Plans in each book.

Time	Topic	Description	Training Technique/ Taxonomy	Materials
	Introduction and Housekeeping			
	Getting Better Acquainted	Choose ice breaker from appendix.	Ice Breaker	Materials given in appendix
	Understanding Parent Partnerships		Independent Activity Flip and Mark: Flip through the books to see the ***Innovations*** in Parent Partnerships (chapters 2-6). *Comprehension*	***Innovations*** infant and toddler books, tabs
	BIG IDEA: Parents are their children's first and most important teachers.	Teachers provide a variety of means to support parents in their important roles.	Discussion Facilitate a brief discussion of the complex role that parents play. *Comprehension*	***Innovations*** infant and toddler books
	Planning for Parent Involvement		Independent Activity, Discussion Plan for Parent Involvement *Application*	Paper, books, pens

	Planning a Parent Event		Independent Activity Plan for Parent Event *Application*	Paper, pens, ***Innovations*** infant and toddler books
	Innovations: BIG IDEAS	Summary and Evaluation	Reflection, Questions, and Answers *Synthesis, Evaluation*	Workshop Evaluations (choose from appendix)
	Follow-up		Modeling, Information Exchange Parent Participation Activities *Application*	Materials for activity/event chosen

Plan for Parent Involvement

Ask the teachers to plan ways during the next month to involve parents in the classroom.

Plan for Parent Event

The teachers plan an event for parents (announcement, explanation, and materials needed list).

Parent-Participation Activities

Plan two parent-participation activities. The teachers implement them in their classrooms and then discuss the outcomes with their mentor/trainer.

● Use ***Innovations***: BIG IDEAS in summary.

Innovations: **BIG IDEAS**

▶ Parents are their child's first and most important teachers.

▶ Teachers can support parents in their important roles.

Curriculum Planning Process

● Complete Preparation Checklist in appendix (page 95).

● Read appropriate sections of books, including pages 34-36 in the infant book and pages 32-36 in the toddler book. (Read these first.) Also read pages 59, 77, 121, 143, 189, 207, 259, 279, 327, 347, 389, and 409 in the infant book and pages 71, 93, 163, 191, 235, 261, 323, 347, 407, 429, 487, and 507 in the toddler book.

Time	Topic	Description	Training Technique/ Taxonomy	Materials
	Introduction and Housekeeping			
	Getting Better Acquainted	Choose ice breaker from appendix.	Ice Breaker	Materials given in appendix
	Understanding the Curriculum Planning Process	Through observations in the classroom, teachers are able to determine what children want and need.	Discussion, Lecture Plan a brief explanation of the curriculum planning model. *Analysis*	Curriculum Planning Process Overhead (page 128)
	Webbing is a technique used in curriculum development.	Webbing can help teachers plan for many possibilities for curriculum ideas.	Discussion Lead a brief discussion of the webs in both books. *Application*	Examples of webs in **Innovations** infant and toddler books
	Webbing shows the flexibility of curriculum planning.		Simulation Presentation by Group Leaders, Webbing Activity *Application, Analysis*	Blank transparency sheets, pens

Innovations: BIG IDEAS Follow-up	Summary and Evaluation	Reflection, Questions, and Answers	Workshop Evaluations (choose from appendix)
		Synthesis, Evaluation	
		Trainer/mentor observes webbing in the classroom.	**Innovations** books, paper, pen/pencil
		Application	

Webbing Activity

Divide the teachers into small groups to practice webbing topics of their choice on transparency sheets. Ask the group leaders to share each group's curriculum web with the whole group.

Webbing in the Classroom

Ask the teachers to create a web and implement some ideas from the web in their classrooms. Ask the teachers to write on the back of the web activities what worked well, what activities need to change, and ways to change the process the next time.

● Use **Innovations**: BIG IDEAS in summary.

Innovations: BIG IDEAS

▶ Through observations in the classroom, teachers are able to determine children's wants and needs.

▶ Webbing identifies possibilities for teachers and children in the classroom.

▶ Teacher observations lead to individualization in the classroom.

Environments

● Complete Preparation Checklist in appendix (page 95).

● Read appropriate sections of books, including *Innovations* in Environments pages 55-57, 118-120, 186-187, 257, 325-326, and 386 in the infant book and pages 67-69, 157-160, 231-234, 319-321, 402-405, and 484-486.

Time	Topic	Description	Training Technique/ Taxonomy	Materials
	Introduction and Housekeeping			
	Getting Better Acquainted	Choose ice breaker from appendix.	Ice Breaker	Materials given in appendix
	Innovations in Environments		Independent Activity Flip and Mark: Flip through books and mark *Innovations* in Environments (chapters 2-6). *Comprehension*	*Innovations* infant and toddler books, tabs
	Characteristics of Infant/Toddler Environments		Review, Discussion Review characteristics found in books. *Comprehension*	*Innovations* books—infant (pages 55-57) and toddler (pages 67-69)
	Understanding Environments for Young Children	Teachers have the responsibility to create, maintain, and refresh the classroom environment.	Discussion, Checklist Environments Activity *Evaluation*	Creating Environments for Young Children—Classroom Checklist Overhead/Handout (page 127)
	Innovations: BIG IDEAS	Summary and Evaluation	Reflection, Questions, and Answers *Synthesis, Evaluation*	Workshop Evaluations (choose from appendix)

Discuss environments for young children. Ask the teachers to complete the Classroom Checklist and write goals for their classrooms.

● Use *Innovations*: BIG IDEAS in summary.

Innovations: BIG IDEAS

▶ Creating, maintaining, and refreshing the classroom environment is the teacher's job.

▶ Environments teach!.

Dramatic Possibilities

● Complete Preparation Checklist in appendix (page 95).

● Read appropriate sections of books, including page 25 and the Dramatic Possibilities in each Possibilities Plan in the infant and toddler books.

Time	Topic	Description	Training Technique/ Taxonomy	Materials
	Introduction and Housekeeping			
	Getting Better Acquainted	Choose ice breaker from appendix.	Ice Breaker	Materials given in appendix
	Understanding Dramatic Possibilities		Individual Activity Flip and Mark: Flip through books and mark the Dramatic Possibilities in the 12 Possibilities Plans. *Comprehension*	***Innovations*** infant and toddler books, tabs
	Creating Dramatic Materials for the Classroom		Independent Activity Teachers can make their toys and bring them to the workshop to share. *Application*	Materials needed to make toys
	Evaluation of Teacher-made Items Before Placing Them in the Classroom		Toy Swap: Teachers switch toys and evaluate them for safety. *Evaluation*	Choke tubes, teacher-made toys

Collecting Dramatic Materials for the Classroom		Communication Note to Parents *Application*	Note to Parents Form (page 138), pens, dictionary
Innovations: BIG IDEAS	Summary and Evaluation	Reflection, Questions, and Answers *Synthesis, Evaluation*	Workshop Evaluations (choose from appendix)

Note to Parents

Ask the teachers to identify materials needed for dramatic possibilities and, using the Note to Parents Form (page 138), write a note to post for parents. Ask the teachers to exchange notes to check for clarity, completeness, spelling, and grammar.

● Use ***Innovations***: BIG IDEAS in summary.

Innovations: **BIG IDEAS**

➧ Teacher-made toys are an important part of the classroom environment.

➧ All materials must be evaluated for appropriateness and safety before being used in the classroom.

➧ Parents can provide valuable resources for the classroom.

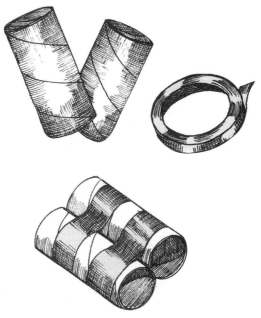

Teacher-made Binoculars

Sensory/Art Possibilities

● Complete Preparation Checklist in appendix (page 95).

● Read appropriate sections of books, including page 25 and the Sensory/Art Possibilities in each Possibility Plan in the infant and toddler books.

READ THIS

Time	Topic	Description	Training Technique/ Taxonomy	Materials
	Introduction and Housekeeping			
	Getting Better Acquainted	Choose ice breaker from appendix.	Ice Breaker	Materials given in appendix
	Understanding Sensory/Art Possibilities		Individual Activity Flip and Mark: Flip through books and mark the Sensory/Art Possibilities in the 12 Possibilities Plans. *Comprehension*	***Innovations*** infant and toddler books, tabs
	Creating Sensory/Art Materials for the Classroom		Independent Activity Teachers can make their toys and bring them to the workshop to share. *Application*	Materials needed to make toys
	Evaluation of Teacher-made Items Before Placing Them in the Classroom		Toy Swap: Teachers switch toys and evaluate them for safety. *Evaluation*	Choke tubes, teacher-made toys

Collecting Sensory/Art Materials for the Classroom		Communication Note to Parents *Application*	Note to Parents Form (page 138), pens, dictionary
Innovations: BIG IDEAS	Summary and Evaluation	Reflection, Questions, and Answers *Synthesis, Evaluation*	Workshop Evaluations (choose from appendix)

Note to Parents

Ask the teachers to identify materials needed for sensory/art possibilities and, using the Note to Parents Form (page 138), write a note to post for parents. Ask the teachers to exchange notes to check for clarity, completeness, spelling, and grammar.

● Use ***Innovations***: BIG IDEAS in summary.

Innovations: **BIG IDEAS**

▶ Teacher-made toys are an important part of the classroom environment.

▶ All materials must be evaluated for appropriateness and safety before being used in the classroom.

▶ Parents can provide valuable resources for the classroom.

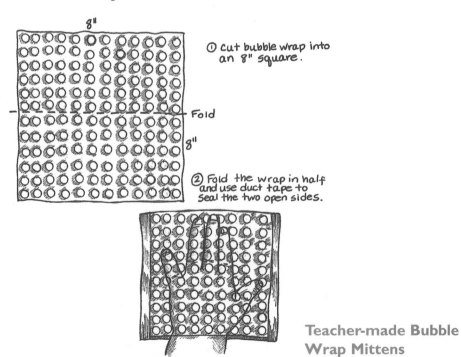

Teacher-made Bubble Wrap Mittens

Curiosity Possibilities

- Complete Preparation Checklist in appendix (page 95).

- Read appropriate sections of books, including pages 25-27 and the Curiosity Possibilities in each Possibility Plan in the infant book and pages 26-27 and the Curiosity Possibilities in each Possibility Plan in the toddler book.

READ THIS

Time	Topic	Description	Training Technique/ Taxonomy	Materials
	Introduction and Housekeeping			
	Getting Better Acquainted	Choose ice breaker from appendix.	Ice Breaker	Materials given in appendix
	Understanding Curiosity Possibilities		Individual Activity Flip and Mark: Flip through books and mark the Curiosity Possibilities in the 12 Possibilities Plans. *Comprehension*	***Innovations*** infant and toddler books, tabs
	Creating Curiosity Materials for the Classroom		Independent Activity Teachers can make their toys and bring them to the workshop to share. *Application*	Materials needed to make toys
	Evaluation of Teacher-made Items Before Placing Them in the Classroom		Toy Swap: Teachers switch toys and evaluate them for safety. *Evaluation*	Choke tubes, teacher-made toys

		Collecting Curiosity Materials for the Classroom		Communication Note to Parents *Application*	Note to Parents Form (page 138), pens, dictionary
		Innovations: BIG IDEAS	Summary and Evaluation	Reflection, Questions, and Answers *Synthesis, Evaluation*	Workshop Evaluations (choose from appendix)

Note to Parents

Ask the teachers to identify materials needed for curiosity possibilities and, using the Note to Parents Form (page 138), write a note to post for parents. Ask the teachers to exchange notes to check for clarity, completeness, spelling, and grammar.

● Use ***Innovations***: BIG IDEAS in summary.

Innovations: **BIG IDEAS**

▶ Teacher-made toys are an important part of the classroom environment.

▶ All materials must be evaluated for appropriateness and safety before being used in the classroom.

▶ Parents can provide valuable resources for the classroom.

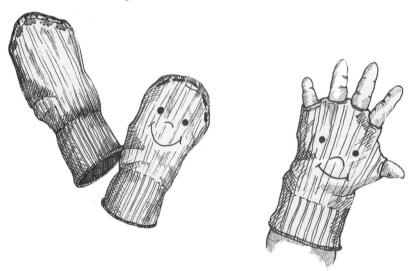

Teacher-made Sock Puppet

Construction Possibilities (for Toddlers)

- Complete Preparation Checklist in appendix (page 95).

- Read appropriate sections of books, including page 27 and the Construction Possibilities in each Possibility Plan in the toddler book.

READ THIS

Time	Topic	Description	Training Technique/ Taxonomy	Materials
	Introduction and Housekeeping			
	Getting Better Acquainted	Choose ice breaker from appendix.	Ice Breaker	Materials given in appendix
	Understanding Construction Possibilities		Individual Activity Flip and Mark: Flip through books and mark the Construction Possibilities in the 12 Possibilities Plans. *Comprehension*	***Innovations*** infant and toddler books, tabs
	Creating Construction Materials for the Classroom		Independent Activity Teachers can make their toys and bring them to the workshop to share. *Application*	Materials needed to make toys
	Evaluation of Teacher-made Items Before Placing Them in the Classroom		Toy Swap: Teachers switch toys and evaluate them for safety. *Evaluation*	Choke tubes, teacher-made toys

| | | Collecting Construction Materials for the Classroom | Summary and Evaluation | Communication

Note to Parents

Application | Note to Parents Form (page 138), pens, dictionary |
| | | ***Innovations***: BIG IDEAS | | Reflection, Questions, and Answers

Synthesis, Evaluation | Workshop Evaluations (choose from appendix) |

Note to Parents

FORMS Ask the teachers to identify materials needed for construction possibilities and, using the Note to Parents Form (page 138), write a note to post for parents. Ask the teachers to exchange notes to check for clarity, completeness, spelling, and grammar.

● Use ***Innovations***: BIG IDEAS in summary.

Innovations: **BIG IDEAS**

▶ Teacher-made toys are an important part of the classroom environment.

▶ All materials must be evaluated for appropriateness and safety before being used in the classroom.

▶ Parents can provide valuable resources for the classroom.

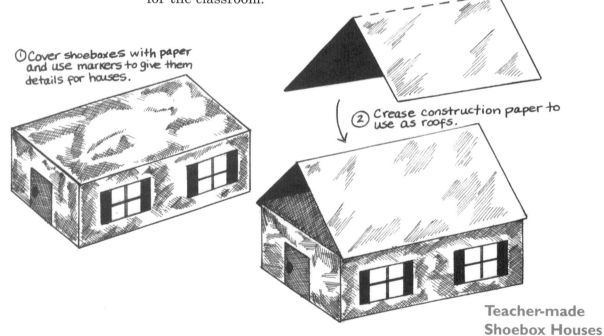

① Cover shoeboxes with paper and use markers to give them details for houses.

② Crease construction paper to use as roofs.

Teacher-made Shoebox Houses

Music/Movement Possibilities

● Complete Preparation Checklist in appendix (page 95).

● Read appropriate sections of books, including pages 27-28 and the Music/Movement Possibilities in each Possibility Plan in the infant book and pages 28-29 and the Music/Movement Possibilities in each Possibility Plan in the toddler book.

Time	Topic	Description	Training Technique/ Taxonomy	Materials
	Introduction and Housekeeping			
	Getting Better Acquainted	Choose ice breaker from appendix.	Ice Breaker	Materials given in appendix
	Understanding Music/ Movement Possibilities		Individual Activity Flip and Mark: Flip through books and mark the Music/Movement Possibilities in the 12 Possibilities Plans. *Comprehension*	***Innovations*** infant and toddler books, tabs
	Creating Music/ Movement Materials for the Classroom		Independent Activity Teachers can make their toys and bring them to the workshop to share. *Application*	Materials needed to make toys
	Evaluation of Teacher-made Items Before Placing Them in the Classroom		Toy Swap: Teachers switch toys and evaluate them for safety. *Evaluation*	Choke tubes, teacher-made toys

Collecting Music/ Movement Materials for the Classroom		Communication Note to Parents *Application*	Note to Parents Form (page 138), pens, dictionary
Innovations: BIG IDEAS	Summary and Evaluation	Reflection, Questions, and Answers *Synthesis, Evaluation*	Workshop Evaluations (choose from appendix)

Note to Parents

Ask the teachers to identify materials needed for music/movement possibilities and, using the Note to Parents Form (page 138), write a note to post for parents. Ask the teachers to exchange notes to check for clarity, completeness, spelling, and grammar.

● Use ***Innovations***: BIG IDEAS in summary.

Innovations: BIG IDEAS

▶ Teacher-made toys are an important part of the classroom environment.

▶ All materials must be evaluated for appropriateness and safety before being used in the classroom.

▶ Parents can provide valuable resources for the classroom.

**Teacher-made
Food Container Rattles**

Literacy Possibilities

● Complete Preparation Checklist in appendix (page 95).

● Read appropriate sections of books, including page 27 and the Literacy Possibilities in each Possibility Plan in the infant book and pages 27-28 and the Possibilities in each Literacy Possibility Plan in the toddler book.

Time	Topic	Description	Training Technique/ Taxonomy	Materials
	Introduction and Housekeeping			
	Getting Better Acquainted	Choose ice breaker from appendix.	Ice Breaker	Materials given in appendix
	Understanding Literacy Possibilities		Individual Activity Flip and Mark: Flip through books and mark the Literacy Possibilities in the 12 Possibilities Plans. *Comprehension*	***Innovations*** infant and toddler books, tabs
	Creating Literacy Materials for the Classroom		Independent Activity Teachers can make their toys/books and bring them to the workshop to share. *Application*	Materials needed to make toys
	Evaluation of Teacher-made Items Before Placing Them in the Classroom		Toy Swap: Teachers switch toys/books and evaluate them for safety. *Evaluation*	Choke tubes, teacher-made toys

Collecting Literacy Materials for the Classroom		Communication Note to Parents *Application*	Note to Parents Form (page 138), pens, dictionary
Innovations: BIG IDEAS	Summary and Evaluation	Reflection, Questions, and Answers *Synthesis, Evaluation*	Workshop Evaluations (choose from appendix)

Note to Parents

Ask the teachers to identify materials needed for literacy possibilities and, using the Note to Parents Form (page 138), write a note to post for parents. Ask the teachers to exchange notes to check for clarity, completeness, spelling, and grammar.

● Use ***Innovations***: BIG IDEAS in summary.

Innovations: BIG IDEAS

▶ Teacher-made toys are an important part of the classroom environment.

▶ All materials must be evaluated for appropriateness and safety before being used in the classroom.

▶ Parents can provide valuable resources for the classroom.

Teacher-made Book

Outdoor Possibilities

● Complete Preparation Checklist in appendix (page 95).

● Read appropriate sections of books, including pages 28, 325-326 and the Outdoor Possibilities in each Possibility Plan in the infant book and pages 29, 402-404 and the Outdoor Possibilities in each Possibility Plan in the toddler book.

Time	Topic	Description	Training Technique/ Taxonomy	Materials
	Introduction and Housekeeping			
	Getting Better Acquainted	Choose ice breaker from appendix.	Ice Breaker	Materials given in appendix
	Understanding Outdoor Possibilities		Individual Activity Flip and Mark: Flip through books and mark the Outdoor Possibilities in the 12 Possibilities Plans. *Comprehension*	***Innovations*** infant and toddler books, tabs
	Creating Outdoor Materials for the Classroom		Independent Activity Teachers can make their toys and bring them to the workshop to share. *Application*	Materials needed to make toys
	Evaluation of Teacher-made Items Before Placing Them in the Classroom		Toy Swap: Teachers switch toys and evaluate them for safety. *Evaluation*	Choke tubes, teacher-made toys

Collecting Outdoor Materials for the Classroom		Communication Note to Parents *Application*	Note to Parents Form (page 138), pens, dictionary
Innovations: BIG IDEAS	Summary and Evaluation	Reflection, Questions, and Answers *Synthesis, Evaluation*	Workshop Evaluations (choose from appendix)

Note to Parents

Ask the teachers to identify materials needed for outdoor possibilities and, using the Note to Parents Form (page 138), write a note to post for parents. Ask the teachers to exchange notes to check for clarity, completeness, spelling, and grammar.

● Use ***Innovations***: BIG IDEAS in summary.

Innovations: BIG IDEAS

➧ Teacher-made toys are an important part of the classroom environment.

➧ All materials must be evaluated for appropriateness and safety before being used in the classroom.

➧ Parents can provide valuable resources for the classroom.

➧ Outdoor play is an important part of good infant and toddler programs.

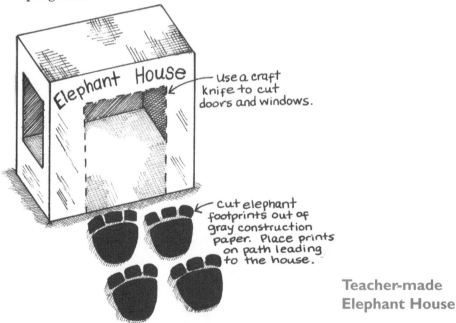

Teacher-made Elephant House

Projects

● Complete Preparation Checklist in appendix (page 95).

● Read appropriate sections of books, including page 28 and the Project Possibilities in each Possibility Plan in the infant book and page 29 and the Project Possibilities in each Possibility Plan in the toddler book.

Time	Topic	Description	Training Technique/ Taxonomy	Materials
	Introduction and Housekeeping			
	Getting Better Acquainted	Choose ice breaker from appendix.	Ice Breaker	Materials given in appendix
	Understanding Projects for Young Children		Individual Activity Flip and Mark: Flip through books and mark the Project Possibilities in the 12 Possibilities Plans. Discuss examples of projects in books. *Comprehension*	***Innovations*** infant and toddler books, tabs
	Projects are repeated activities or experiences that stretch over a period of time.		Independent Activity, Small Group Activities to Projects *Synthesis*	Project Worksheet Overhead/Handout (page 153)
	Innovations: BIG IDEAS		Reflection, Questions, and Answers *Synthesis, Evaluation*	Workshop Evaluations (choose from appendix)
	Follow-up	Summary and Evaluation	Project Implementation *Application, Evaluation*	Materials necessary for chosen project

Activities to Projects

Discuss how projects are experiences that children have over time. These help children to practice and perfect skills, as well as feel a sense of continuity. Ask the teachers to take activities and translate them into projects. Ask them to share project ideas in groups.

Project Implementation

Ask the teachers to implement a project in their classroom and evaluate it before the next workshop.

● Use *Innovations*: BIG IDEAS in summary.

Innovations: **BIG IDEAS**

▶ Projects provide opportunities to represent ideas and practice and perfect techniques.

Project Possibility: Repeated Foot Painting

Prop Boxes

● Complete Preparation Checklist in appendix (page 95).

● Read appropriate sections of books, including suggestions included under Resources in all infant and toddler Possibility Plans.

READ THIS

Time	Topic	Description	Training Technique/ Taxonomy	Materials
	Introduction and Housekeeping			
	Getting Better Acquainted	Choose ice breaker from appendix.	Ice Breaker	Materials given in appendix
	Understanding Prop Boxes		Individual Activity Flip and Mark: Flip through books and mark the prop box ideas in the 12 Possibilities Plans. *Comprehension*	***Innovations*** infant and toddler books, tabs
	Creating Prop Boxes for the Classroom		Independent Activity Teachers can make their prop boxes and bring them to the workshop to share. *Application*	Materials needed to make prop boxes
	Evaluation of Teacher-made Items Before Placing Them in the Classroom		Prop Box Swap: Teachers switch prop boxes and evaluate them for safety. *Evaluation*	Choke tubes, prop boxes

	Collecting Prop Box Materials for the Classroom		Investigation, Communication Note to Parents *Application*	Note to Parents Form (page 138), pens, dictionary
	Innovations: BIG IDEAS	Summary and Evaluation	Reflection, Questions, and Answers *Synthesis, Evaluation*	Workshop Evaluations (choose from appendix)
	Follow-up		Prop Box Implementation *Application, Evaluation*	Materials necessary for chosen project

Note to Parents

Ask the teachers to identify materials needed for prop boxes and, using the Note to Parents Form (page 138), write a note to post for parents. Ask the teachers to exchange notes to check for clarity, completeness, spelling, and grammar.

Prop Box Implementation

Ask the teachers to implement a prop box in their classroom and evaluate it before the next workshop.

● Use ***Innovations***: BIG IDEAS in summary.

Innovations: **BIG IDEAS**

➡ Teacher-made materials are an important part of the classroom environment.

➡ All materials must be evaluated for appropriateness and safety before being used in the classroom.

➡ Parents can provide valuable resources for the classroom.

➡ Prop boxes provide play cues to children.

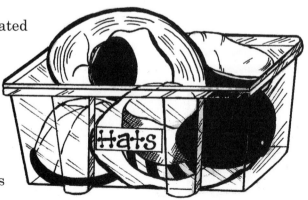

Picture Files/Vocabulary

● Complete Preparation Checklist in appendix (page 95).

● Read appropriate sections of books, including page 29 (infant book) and page 31-32 (toddler book) and all Picture File/Vocabulary suggestions listed in the Resources section for each Possibility Plan.

Time	Topic	Description	Training Technique/ Taxonomy	Materials
	Introduction and Housekeeping			
	Getting Better Acquainted	Choose ice breaker from appendix.	Ice Breaker	Materials given in appendix
	Understanding Picture Files/Vocabulary		Individual Activity Flip and Mark: Flip through books and mark the picture file/vocabulary ideas in the 12 Possibilities Plans. Discuss and examine examples of picture files/vocabulary. *Comprehension*	***Innovations*** infant and toddler books, examples of picture files/vocabulary
	Creating Picture Files/Vocabulary for the Classroom		Competency Building Activity Teachers create picture files and vocabulary cards. *Application*	File folders, index cards, magazines, travel brochures, newspapers, clear contact paper
	Innovations: BIG IDEAS	Summary and Evaluation	Reflection, Questions, and Answers *Synthesis, Evaluation*	Workshop Evaluations (choose from appendix)

● Use *Innovations*: BIG IDEAS in summary.

Innovations: BIG IDEAS

▶ Pictures have meaning.

▶ Picture files support language and cognitive development.

▶ Cultural picture files explore diversity.

Guidance and Discipline

● Complete Preparation Checklist in appendix (page 95).

● Read appropriate sections of books, including Natural and Logical
Consequences on page 315, Setting Appropriate Limits on pages 315-317,
and Teaching Social Problem-solving on pages 171-173 in the infant book
and Managing Normal Aggression in Very Young Children on pages 462-
463 and Dealing with Oppositional Behavior on pages 463-467 in the
toddler book.

READ THIS

Time	Topic	Description	Training Technique/ Taxonomy	Materials
	Introduction and Housekeeping			
	Getting Better Acquainted	Choose ice breaker from appendix.	Ice Breaker	Materials given in appendix
	Understanding Guidance and Discipline	Often the solution for guidance and discipline can be found through research and a problem-solving technique.	Discussion Discuss guidance and discipline as a process. *Comprehension*	
	Ask teachers to bring guidance and discipline concerns with them to the workshop.		Discussion Teachers share concerns in groups. *Knowledge, Comprehension*	Teachers' guidance and discipline concerns that they brought to the workshop

Problem-solving Guidance and Discipline Issues		Discussion, Problem-solving Teachers use problem-solving worksheets individually. Teachers complete definition and research sections of handout. *Knowledge, Comprehension, Application*	Problem-solving Worksheet Overhead/ Handout (page 152)
Brainstorming Solutions to Guidance and Discipline Problems		Brainstorming Teachers brainstorm solutions in groups. *Analysis, Synthesis*	
Creating Action Plans for the Classroom		Teachers decide specific action plan and plan for follow-up. *Analysis, Synthesis, Evaluation*	
		Discussion Teachers share their plans with their groups.	
Innovations: BIG IDEAS	Summary and Evaluation	Reflection, Questions, and Answers *Synthesis, Evaluation*	Workshop Evaluations (choose from appendix)
Follow-up		Trainer/director monitors progress.	

● Use ***Innovations***: BIG IDEAS in summary.

Innovations: BIG IDEAS

▶ Guidance is preventative—what a teacher does before there is a problem.

▶ Discipline teaches self-control.

Biting

● Complete Preparation Checklist in appendix (page 95).

● Read appropriate sections of books, including Handling Biting in the Classroom on pages 173-176 in the infant book and Handling Biting in the Classroom on pages 136-137 in the toddler book to fully understand the three types of biting.

Time	Topic	Description	Training Technique/ Taxonomy	Materials
	Introduction and Housekeeping			
	Getting Better Acquainted	Choose ice breaker from appendix.	Ice Breaker	Materials given in appendix
	Understanding When Young Children Bite	Often the solution for biting can be found through research and a problem-solving technique.	Discussion Discuss guidance and discipline as a process. *Comprehension*	
			Discussion Teachers share concerns in groups. *Knowledge, Comprehension*	Chart paper and markers to write down teachers' concerns about biting
	Problem-solving Biting Issues		Discussion Teachers use problem-solving worksheet individually. Teachers complete definition and research sections of handout. *Knowledge, Comprehension, Application*	Problem-solving Worksheet Overhead/ Handout (page 152)

Brainstorming Solutions to Biting Problems	Summary and Evaluation	Brainstorming Teachers brainstorm solutions in groups. *Analysis, Synthesis*	
Creating Action Plans for the Classroom		Discussion Teachers decide a specific action plan and plan for follow-up. Teachers share their plans with their groups. *Analysis, Synthesis, Evaluation*	
Innovations: BIG IDEAS		Reflection, Questions, and Answers *Synthesis, Evaluation*	Workshop Evaluations (choose from appendix)
Follow-up		Trainer/director monitors progress.	

● Use ***Innovations***: BIG IDEAS in summary.

Innovations: **BIG IDEAS**

➧ Biting is a normal part of development.

➧ Children bite at different stages of development for different reasons.

Aggression

● Complete Preparation Checklist in appendix (page 95).

● Read appropriate sections of books, including Managing Normal Aggression in Very Young Children on pages 374-375 in the infant book and Managing Normal Aggression in Very Young Children on pages 462-463 in the toddler book.

Time	Topic	Description	Training Technique/ Taxonomy	Materials
	Introduction and Housekeeping			
	Getting Better Acquainted	Choose ice breaker from appendix.	Ice Breaker	Materials given in appendix
	Understanding Aggression in Young Children	Often the solution for aggression can be found through research and a problem-solving technique.	Discussion Discuss and understand aggression as a process. *Comprehension*	
			Discussion Teachers share their concerns in groups. *Knowledge, Comprehension*	Chart paper and markers to write down teachers' concerns about aggression
	Problem-solving Aggression Issues		Discussion Teachers use problem-solving worksheet individually. Teachers complete definition and research sections of handout. *Knowledge, Comprehension, Application*	Problem-solving Worksheet Overhead/ Handout (page 152)

	Brainstorming Solutions to Aggression Problems		Brainstorming Teachers brainstorm solutions in groups. *Analysis, Synthesis*	
	Creating Action Plans for the Classroom		Discussion Teachers decide a specific action plan and plan for follow-up. Teachers share their plans with their groups. *Analysis, Synthesis, Evaluation*	
	Innovations: BIG IDEAS	Summary and Evaluation	Reflection, Questions, and Answers *Synthesis, Evaluation*	Workshop Evaluations (choose from appendix)
	Follow-up		Trainer/director monitors progress.	

● Use ***Innovations***: BIG IDEAS in summary.

Innovations: BIG IDEAS

▶ Aggression is a normal part of development.

▶ Children gain skills in regulating emotions.

Social Problem-solving

● Complete Preparation Checklist in appendix (page 95).

● Read appropriate sections of books, including Teaching Social Problem-solving on pages 171-173 in the infant book and Teaching Social Interaction Skills on pages 137-138 in the toddler book.

Time	Topic	Description	Training Technique/ Taxonomy	Materials
	Introduction and Housekeeping			
	Getting Better Acquainted	Choose ice breaker from appendix.	Ice Breaker	Materials given in appendix
	Understanding Social Problem-solving in Young Children	Often the solution for social problem-solving issues can be found through research and a problem-solving technique.	Discussion Discuss social problem-solving as a process. *Comprehension*	
			Discussion Teachers share their concerns in groups. *Knowledge, Comprehension*	Chart paper and markers to write down teachers' social problem-solving concerns
	Problem-solving Aggression Issues		Discussion Teachers use problem-solving worksheet individually. Teachers complete definition and research sections of handout. *Knowledge, Comprehension, Application*	Problem-solving Worksheet Overhead/ Handout (page 152)

		Brainstorming Solutions to Aggression Problems		Brainstorming Teachers brainstorm solutions in groups. Analysis, Synthesis	
		Creating Action Plans for the Classroom		Discussion Teachers decide a specific action plan and plan for follow-up. Teachers share their plans with their groups. *Analysis, Synthesis, Evaluation*	
		Innovations: BIG IDEAS	Summary and Evaluation	Reflection, Questions, and Answers *Synthesis, Evaluation*	Workshop Evaluations (choose from appendix)
		Follow-up		Trainer/director monitors progress.	

● Use ***Innovations***: BIG IDEAS in summary.

Innovations: **BIG IDEAS**

▶ Children can learn social problem-solving in the classroom.

Toileting

● Complete Preparation Checklist in appendix (page 95).

● Read appropriate sections of books, including pages 371-373, 375-378, and 393-398 in the toddler book.

READ THIS

Time	Topic	Description	Training Technique/ Taxonomy	Materials
	Introduction and Housekeeping			
	Getting Better Acquainted	Choose ice breaker from appendix.	Ice Breaker	Materials given in appendix
	Understanding Toileting as a Process for Toddlers		Reading, Discussion Teachers read appropriate pages in the toddler book and discuss any questions they have. *Knowledge, Comprehension, Application, Analysis*	***Innovations*** toddler books
	Teachers and parents are partners in teaching children to toilet.		Discussion Teachers make a plan for working with parents to begin the toilet-training process for a child in the classroom. Include how they will use parent postcards in the process. *Analysis, Synthesis*	

			Discussion	
			Teachers share their plans in groups and offer suggestions.	
			Analysis, Synthesis, Evaluation	
	Innovations: BIG IDEAS	Summary and Evaluation	Reflection, Questions, and Answers	Workshop Evaluations (choose from appendix)
			Synthesis, Evaluation	

● Use ***Innovations***: BIG IDEAS in summary.

Innovations: **BIG IDEAS**

▶ Learning to toilet is a developmental process.

▶ Each stage in toilet training builds on the previous stage.

Portfolios

● Complete Preparation Checklist in appendix (page 95).

● Read appropriate sections of books, including page 107 in the infant book.

READ THIS

Time	Topic	Description	Training Technique/ Taxonomy	Materials
	Introduction and Housekeeping			
	Getting Better Acquainted	Choose ice breaker from appendix.	Ice Breaker	Materials given in appendix
	Preparing Children's Portfolios		Individual Activity Search and Find *Comprehension, Application*	***Innovations*** infant and toddler books, paper, pens
			Documentation Planning Portfolio Plan *Analysis, Synthesis*	List of potential entries in the child's portfolio, Portfolio Planning Form (page 147), paper, pens
	Innovations: BIG IDEAS	Summary and Evaluation	Reflection, Questions, and Answers *Synthesis, Evaluation*	Workshop Evaluations (choose from appendix)

Search and Find

Ask the teachers to search the infant and toddler curriculum books to create a list of potential entries in the portfolio.

Portfolio Plan

FORMS

Ask the teachers to use the list generated above to create a plan for portfolios for the children in their class using the Portfolio Planning Form Handout (page 147). Ask them to identify what all the portfolios will have in them, and to identify ways to make each portfolio unique and reflect the individual child.

● Use *Innovations*: BIG IDEAS in summary.

Innovations: BIG IDEAS

▶ Portfolios document children's growth and development.

Appendix

Preparation Checklist
(Check item when completed)

_____ Secure place and calendar date for the event.

_____ Order books for teachers (if needed).

_____ Communicate the training place, time, and topic.

_____ Read the appropriate sections of books. (Page numbers are listed on each module.)

_____ Secure materials needed (see materials column on grid).

_____ Copy handouts (see materials column on grid).

_____ Copy overhead transparencies (see materials column on grid). Punch holes in them and place them in a three-ring binder.

_____ Arrange for rolls, coffee, lunch, and breaks.

_____ Prepare training certificates.

_____ Fill in times on training grid to reflect the length and type of training workshop.

Items I need to copy for overhead transparencies and handouts:

Items I need to gather/purchase:

Notes

12 Learning Tasks: Simplified Piaget by Alice Honig

INNOVATIONS

Alice Honig, a noted early childhood specialist, simplifies Piaget's theories by synthesizing the learning tasks of childhood into 12 categories (Honig, 1982). Some teachers will find that they already spend an enormous amount of time exposing children to these learning tasks. Each should be incorporated in planned interactions with children throughout the day.

1. Learning to make groups
2. Learning to separate parts from the big group
3. Learning to line up objects in a logical order
4. Learning time relationships
5. Learning about places and how space is organized
6. Learning what numbers mean
7. Learning to recognize change
8. Learning to use body parts together
9. Learning to reason
10. Learning to use imagination
11. Learning language and using books
12. Learning social skills

Understanding these learning tasks of the first three years allows teachers to capitalize on emerging skills by developing appropriate curriculum plans. Each of these tasks offers numerous opportunities to enhance the intellectual development of very young children.

Accident/Incident Report

Name of injured child

Date of accident/incident

Location of accident (address)

Site (place in school)

What happened? Describe what took place.

Why did it happen? Give all of the facts—why? where? what? when? who? etc.

What should be done to prevent this accident from recurring?

If the accident involved a child, how were the parents notified and by whom?

What was the parent's reaction?

What has been done so far to correct the situation?

With whom was this accident discussed, other than the child's parents?

Reported by   Date

Anecdotal Record

Child _____ **Date** _____ **Time** _____

What I observed
_____
_____
_____
_____
_____
_____
_____
_____
_____
_____
_____

Teacher _____

Anecdotal Record

Child _____ **Date** _____ **Time** _____

What I observed
_____
_____
_____
_____
_____
_____
_____
_____
_____
_____
_____

Teacher _____

Anecdotal Record—Example of Anetria

Anecdotal Record

Child Anetria   **Date** 11/14/00   **Time** 10:15 am

What I observed   Seth and Anetria are playing in the dramatic play area. There are two prop boxes out in the area—one is the firefighter prop box and the other is the hats prop box. Anetria has the firefighter's hat on her head and is pulling the hoses (made of short pieces of garden hose) out of the firefighter's prop box. Seth is watching what Anetria is doing. After watching for about 2 minutes, Seth goes over and pulls the hat off of Anetria's head. She looks at him and says "My hat." He turns and walks away, picking up a hose piece on the way. Anetria screams, begins to cry, and jumps up and down. The teacher, Ms. Brenda, comes over to the dramatic play area, kneels down at Anetria's eye level, and asks Anetria, "What's wrong?" Anetria continues to cry and points to Seth, saying "He took my hat!" Brenda says, "Did you want him to take it?" She says, "No!" Brenda says, "Then let's go tell him." She takes Anetria by the hand and walks her over to Seth. She says to Seth, "Seth, Anetria has a problem she wants to discuss with you." Seth turns and looks at Brenda. Brenda kneels by Anetria, looks at her and says, "Tell him your problem." Anetria says, "That mine," pointing to the hat. Seth says, "No, it's not, it's mine." Anetria begins to cry again. Brenda says to Anetria, "I don't think crying is working. Tell Seth you want the hat back." Anetria says "Back." Seth says "No!" Brenda looks at Anetria and says, "See if he will trade another hat for the firefighter's hat." Anetria goes over to the hat prop box, gets another hat (a cowboy hat) and hands it to Seth. Seth takes it and hands Anetria the firefighter's hat. Brenda says to Anetria, "When you are finished with the firefighter's hat, check with Seth to see if he wants to play with it." Anetria nods and goes back to dramatic play, swooshing her hose.

Teacher Ms. Woods

Arrow Curriculum Graphic

Developmental Tasks

Observations and Assessment

Child Development

Interactive Experiences

Teaching

Parent Participation and Involvement

Environment

Activities and Experiences

Books Read List

Book Title	Date
1.	
2.	
3.	
4.	
5.	
6.	
7.	
8.	
9.	
10.	
11.	
12.	
13.	
14.	
15.	
16.	
17.	
18.	
19.	
20.	
21.	
22.	
23.	
24.	
25.	
26.	
27.	
28.	
29.	
30.	

Communication Sheet

CHILD'S NAME _____ **FOR THE WEEK OF** _____

DAY	BREAKFAST		TOTAL HOURS SLEPT	BEHAVIOR CHANGES NOTICED		PARENT COMMENTS/INSTRUCTIONS	FOODS EATEN		DIAPER CHANGES		NAPTIME		TEACHER COMMENTS
	YES	NO		YES	NO		SOLIDS	LIQUIDS	WET	BM	START	WOKE	
M													
T													
W													
Th													
F													

Complete List of BIG IDEAS

- Development is integrated across four domains—physical, intellectual, emotional, and social.
- The younger the child, the more we see overlap in the domains of physical, intellectual, emotional, and social development.
- Developmental tasks are a new way to conceptualize how children grow and learn.
- Understanding child development leads to understanding behaviors.
- Interactions matter!
- Routines ARE interactions.
- Begin everything with observation.
- Parents are their child's first and most important teachers.
- Create partnerships with parents.
- Teachers can support parents in their important roles.
- Environments teach!
- Webbing opens up possibilities.
- Planning is preparation for interactions.
- Children are always learning through their experiences.
- Teachers need numerous resources and can make many of them.
- Infant and toddler behavior often has a developmental explanation.
- Age is a poor predictor of developmental stage.
- Doing a developmental skill first (or last) is not related to potential or future outcomes.
- Attachment is a process important to a child's development.
- Separation anxiety is an integral part of the attachment process.
- Stranger anxiety shows progress in the attachment process.
- Children are born with personality types (fearful, flexible, feisty).
- All children (even happy, flexible ones) need attention from caring adults.
- Children learn through play—through the active exploration of materials.
- Children participate in different types of play in different environments.
- Observing children at play reveals developmental information.
- Children and adults learn by using multiple intelligences.
- Reading books to children stimulates both language and cognitive skills.
- Intelligence is the result of a complex relationship between genes and experiences.

Complete List of BIG IDEAS (continued)

- The size of a toddler's vocabulary is a direct result of how much the teacher talks with him or her.
- Teachers can support early literacy.
- Conflicts/problems are a common outgrowth of play.
- Conflicts are an opportunity to teach social problem solving.
- Teachers observe and assess before they know what experiences are appropriate.
- Ping-ponging shows mutual respect between teacher and child.
- Through observations in the classroom, teachers are able to determine children's wants/needs.
- Webbing identifies possibilities for teachers and children in the classroom.
- Teacher observations lead to individualization in the classroom.
- Creating, maintaining, and refreshing the classroom environment is the teacher's job.
- Teacher-made materials are an important part of the classroom environment.
- All materials must be evaluated for appropriateness and safety before being used in the classroom.
- Parents can provide valuable resources for the classroom.
- Outdoor play is an important part of good infant and toddler programs.
- Projects provide opportunities to represent ideas and to practice and perfect techniques.
- Prop boxes provide play cues to children.
- Pictures have meaning.
- Picture files support language and cognitive development.
- Cultural picture files explore diversity.
- Guidance is preventative—what a teacher does before there is a problem.
- Discipline teaches self-control.
- Biting is a normal part of development.
- Children bite for different reasons at different stages in their development.
- Aggression is a normal part of development.
- Children gain skills in regulating emotions.
- Children can learn social problem-solving in the classroom.
- Learning to toilet is a developmental process.
- Each stage in toilet training builds on the previous stage.
- Portfolios document children's growth and development.

Innovations
Complete
Observation/Assessment
Birth to 18 Months

CHILD'S NAME   TEACHER

Infant (0-18 months) Assessment

Task: Separating from Parents

	0-6 months	6-12 months		12-18 months
S1	a. Little or no experience with separating from Mom and Dad; accepts sensitive care from substitute.	b. Some experience with separating from Mom and Dad; prefers familiar caregiver, but accepts sensitive care from substitute.	c. More experience with separating from Mom and Dad; resists separating; shows distress upon separation, and takes time to adjust.	d. Experienced with separating from Mom and Dad; resists initial separation, but adjusts after only a few moments.
S2	a. Startled by new sounds, smells, and people.	b. Orients toward new or interesting stimuli.		c. Seeks new and interesting stimuli.
S3	a. Accepts transitions without notice.	b. Reacts with discomfort during the transition.	c. Resists transition preparation as well as the transition.	d. Anticipates transitions when preparation activities begin. If preparation is to a preferred, familiar activity, transition is accepted.
S4	a. Displays indiscriminate attachment; will accept sensitive care from most familiar adults; exhibits preference for Mom, Dad, or familiar caregiver if present.	b. Displays discriminate attachment; will still accept care from sensitive caregivers, but prefers care from Mom, Dad, or familiar caregivers.		c. Separation anxiety emerges; resists approaches by unfamiliar adults and resists separation from Mom, Dad, and familiar caregivers. Cries, clings, calls for parents when they leave the child's view.
S5	a. Unpredictable daily schedule.	b. Patterns in daily schedule emerge around eating and sleeping.		c. Daily schedule is predictable. Eating and sleeping patterns are relatively stable and predictable.
S6	a. Feeds from breast or bottle.	b. Begins to take baby food from a spoon; begins to sip from a cup.		c. Drinks from bottle and/or cup; eats finger foods.
S7	a. Plays with objects within visual field; bats at objects with hands and feet.	b. Manipulates, mouths, and plays with objects; likes action/reaction toys. Plays with objects then drops them to move on to new objects. May return to objects again and again.		c. Plays with favorite things again and again. Likes to dump out objects and play with them on the floor. Considers all objects and toys in the environment personal play choices, even when being played with by others.

Infant (0-18 months) Assessment

Task: Connecting with School and Teacher

	0-6 months		6-12 months	12-18 months
C1	a. Does not resist separating from parents.		b. Resists separating from parents; resists comfort from primary teacher.	c. Resists separating from parents; accepts comfort from primary teacher.
C2	a. Accepts transition from parent to teacher.		b. Maintains physical proximity to primary teacher during separation.	c. Seeks primary teacher's support in separating.
C3	a. Comforts after a period of distress.		b. Comforts quickly after being picked up.	c. Comforts when needs or wants are acknowledged by caregiver.
C4	a. Is unaware of friends in classroom.		b. Visually notices friends in classroom.	c. Gets excited about seeing friends; seeks physical proximity.
C5	a. Uses parents and teacher physically to support exploration of the environment; explores objects placed nearby parents and teachers.		b. Uses parents and teacher visually to support exploration of the environment; manipulates objects found in environment.	c. Explores the environment independently; responds to play cues presented by adults.
C6	a. Focuses on face-to-face interaction.	b. Tracks moving object up and down and right to left.	c. Watches people, objects, and activities in immediate environment.	d. Initiates interactions with people, toys, and the environment.
C7	a. Objects exist only when in view.	b. Objects perceived as having separate existence.	c. Looks where objects were last seen after they disappear.	d. Follows visual displacement of objects.
C8	a. Thinks object disappears when it moves out of view.	b. Looks where object was last seen after it disappears.	c. Follows object as it disappears.	d. Searches for hidden object if the disappearance was observed.

Infant (0-18 months) Assessment

Task: Relating to Self and Others

	0-6 months	6-12 months		12-18 months
R1	a. Calms self with adult support.	b. Calms self with support from adults and/or transitional objects.		c. Calms self with transitional objects.
R2	a. Unaware of own image in mirror.	b. Curious about own image in mirrors and photographs.	c. Discovers self in mirror and photographs.	d. Differentiates own image from images of others.
R3	a. Begins to demonstrate preferences for different types of sensory stimuli.	b. Prefers some types of stimuli to others.		c. Is interested in pursuing favorite stimulation activities again and again.
R4	a. Develops a multi-sensory interest in the world—wants to see, touch, mouth, hear, and hold objects.	b. Uses senses to explore and discover the near environment.		c. Uses motor movements to enhance sensory exploration of the environment.
R5	a. Play is predominantly unoccupied in nature.	b. Play is predominantly onlooker in nature.	c. Play is predominantly solitary in nature.	
R6	a. Exhibits practice play.			b. Exhibits symbolic play.
R7	a. Develops an interest in the human world.	b. Seeks interactions with responsive adults; interested also in what other children are doing.	c. Seeks most interactions with familiar adults; fascinated by what other children are doing.	d. Prefers interactions with familiar adults; resists interaction with unfamiliar adults; may be cautious with unfamiliar friends.
R8	a. Does not distinguish between needs (social interaction, a new position, holding instead of lying in the bed) and wants (food, diaper changes, sleep).	b. Begins to distinguish between needs and wants; can communicate differently about different needs and wants.	c. Uses objects, gestures, and behaviors to indicate needs and wants.	d. Uses single words to indicate needs and wants like "muk" for "I want milk," or "bye-bye" for "Let's go bye-bye."
R9	a. Creates mental images of emotions and emotional responses to situations.			b. Begins to understand how feelings relate to others.
R10	a. Unable to negotiate interactions with peers without direct adult support and facilitation.	b. Calls for help loudly by crying or screaming when problems occur during exploration of the environment or with peers.	c. Exchanges or trades with peers to get a desired toy or material with direct adult support and facilitation.	d. Asks other children to walk away when conflict arises between children; expects the other child to do so.
R11	a. Explores environment and the things in it orally. May bite, poke, scratch, or pinch others during exploration.			b. Experiments with behavior that gets a reaction; may bite, pinch, poke, scratch during interactions with others to see what happens.

Infant (0-18 months) Assessment

Task: Communicating with Parents, Teachers, and Friends

	0-6 months			6-12 months		12-18 months
CM1	a. Gazes at familiar faces.	b. Responds to facial expressions of familiar faces.	c. Occasionally engages in reciprocal communication with facial expressions, vowel sounds, and voice inflection.	d. Frequently engages in reciprocal communication using facial expressions, inflection, and vowel and consonant sounds.		e. Imitates and jabbers in response to familiar voices.
CM2	a. Makes sounds.	b. Imitates intonational and inflectional vocal patterns.		c. Develops holophrasic speech—words that convey complete sentences or thoughts.	d. Uses the same word to convey different meaning.	e. Develops telegraphic speech, where 2 or 3 words are used as a sentence.
CM3	a. Listens to familiar people's voices when they talk.	b. Shows understanding of simple phrases by responding or reacting.		c. Points to or looks at familiar objects when asked to do so.		d. Follows commands with visual cues or context cues.
CM4	a. Babbles motorically, acoustically, and visually simple sounds like (m), (p), (b), (n) at the beginning of words and vowel sounds like (ah), (oh), (uh).			b. Babbles sounds like (w), (k), (f), (t), (d) at the beginning of words and vowels sounds like (eh), (ee); strings sounds together (ba-ba-ba-ba-ba) and practices sounds in a wide variety of ways.		
CM5	a. Responds discriminantly to voices of mother and father.	b. Turns toward and responds to familiar voices and sounds.		c. Prefers familiar sounds and voices.		d. Directs vocalizations toward familiar people and objects in the environment.
CM6	a. Experiments with babbling and cooing.	b. Inflection is added to babbling and cooing.				c. Single words or phrases are understandable to familiar adults; strangers may not understand these words.
CM7	a. Looks at picture books.	b. Listens to books when read by a familiar adult.			c. Points to pictures.	d. Turns pages.

Task: *Moving Around Home and School*

	0-6 months					6-12 months					12-18 months					
M1	a. Holds head away from shoulder.	b. Holds head steady side to side.	c. Holds head up when lying on stomach.	d. Rolls from back to front.	e. Rolls from front to back.	f. Scoots on stomach.	g. Sits with support.	h. Sits without support.	i. Crawls after ball or toy.	j. Pulls to a stand.	k. Lowers back down to squatting position.	l. Walks with support.	m. Walks without support.	n. Squats down and stands back up.	o. Climbs into chair.	p. Kicks ball.
M2	a. Eyes and head follow motion.	b. Holds rattle.	c. Exchanges objects between hands.	d. Uses pincher grasp to pick up small items.	e. Picks up toys and objects.	f. Dumps objects out of containers.	g. Puts objects back into containers.	h. Scribbles.			i. Turns pages in cardboard book.	j. Unbuttons large buttons.	k. Completes puzzles with 2-3 pieces.			

Infant (0-18 months) Assessment

Task: Expressing Feelings with Parents, Teachers, and Friends

	0-6 months	**6-12 months**	**12-18 months**
E1	a. Begins to self-regulate; calms self after sensitive response from a caring adult.	b. Expects adults to respond to social cues such as vocalization, gestures, or cries.	c. Knows which behaviors will make caregivers react in certain ways (for example, which actions will make you laugh and which ones will make you say "stop").
E2	a. Develops an interest in the world; is alert to sounds, touch, and faces.	b. Explores the environment; picks up objects of interest, then moves on to other objects.	c. Plays in a focused, organized manner.
E3	a. Gazes at faces with interest; smiles responsively.	b. Reaches up to indicate an interest in being held; is interested in social interaction with familiar adults.	c. Uses physical behavior (such as crawling over and pulling up) to establish closeness to caregivers.
E4	a. Seeks interactions with familiar people; vocalizes in response to vocalization.	b. Seeks to explore interesting toys, objects, and people.	c. Responds to limits that are set verbally; complies only with support from adults.
E5	a. Emotional reactions continue for a minute or two after an adult responds; does not recognize the change in state immediately.	b. Begins to coordinate behavior and emotions by acting on feelings; connects physical actions with needs (for example, goes over to the refrigerator to indicate interest in food or drink).	c. Recovers from emotional outbursts in a few minutes most of the time.

Infant (0-18 months) Observation and Assessment Summary

	0-6 months		6-12 months		12-18 months	
	Subtask	Date	Subtask	Date	Subtask	Date
Task 1 **Separating from** **Parents**	S1a		S1b		S1d	
			S1c			
	S2a		S2b		S2c	
	S3a		S3b		S3d	
			S3c			
	S4a		S4b		S4c	
	S5a		S5b		S5c	
	S6a		S6b		S6c	
	S7a		S7b		S7c	
Task 2 **Connecting with** **School and Teacher**	C1a		C1b		C1c	
	C2a		C2b		C2c	
	C3a		C3b		C3c	
	C4a		C4b		C4c	
	C5a		C5b		C5c	
	C6a		C6c		C6d	
	C6b					
	C7a		C7c		C7d	
	C7b					
	C8a		C8c		C8d	
	C8b					
Task 3 **Relating to Self and** **Others**	R1a		R1b		R1c	
	R2a		R2b		R2d	
			R2c			
	R3a		R3b		R3c	
	R4a		R4b		R4c	
	R5a		R5b		R5c	
			R5c			
	R6a		R6a		R6b	
	R7a		R7b		R7d	
			R7c			
	R8a		R8b		R8d	
			R8c			
	R9a		R9a		R9b	
	R10a		R10b		R10d	
			R10c			
	R11a		R11a		R11b	

	0-6 months		6-12 months		12-18 months	
	Subtask	Date	Subtask	Date	Subtask	Date
Task 4 **Communicating** **with Parents,** **Teachers, and Friends**	CM1a		CM1d		CM1e	
	CM1b					
	CM1c					
	CM2a		CM2c		CM2e	
	CM2b		CM2d			
	CM3a		CM3c		CM3d	
	CM3b					
	CM4a		CM4b		CM4b	
	CM5a		CM5c		CM5d	
	CM5b					
	CM6a		CM6b		CM6c	
	CM6b					
	CM7a		CM7b		CM7c	
	CM7b				CM7d	
Task 5 **Moving around** **Home and School**	M1a		M1f		M1k	
	M1b		M1g		M1l	
	M1c		M1h		M1m	
	M1d		M1i		M1n	
	M1e		M1j		M1o	
					M1p	
	M2a		M2e		M2i	
	M2b		M2f		M2j	
	M2c		M2g		M2k	
	M2d		M2h			
Task 6 **Expressing Feelings** **with Parents,** **Teachers, and Friends**	E1a		E1b		E1c	
	E2a		E2b		E2c	
	E3a		E3b		E3c	
	E4a		E4b		E4c	
	E5a		E5b		E5c	

Innovations
Complete
Observation/Assessment
18 to 36 Months

CHILD'S NAME

TEACHER

Toddler (18-36 months) Assessment

Task: Transitioning to School

	18-24 months	24-30 months		30-36 months
T1	a. Experienced in separating from Mom and Dad; may resist initial separation in new or unusual settings, but adjusts after a few moments.	b. Experienced with separating; looks forward to favorite activities. May approach new or unusual settings with caution, but gets interested after a few minutes.		c. Separates easily in most situations. If cautious, gets over caution quickly when invited to join in by a friendly adult or peer.
T2	a. Actively seeks new and interesting stimuli; interested in everything in the environment.	b. May get into difficulty seeking and exploring interesting stimuli (e.g., climbing on furniture, opening off-limits cabinets).		c. Seeks novel and interesting stimuli; when presented with familiar and novel stimuli, prefers novel ones.
T3	a. Resists separations and transitions to unfamiliar or new settings or to settings that are not preferred.	b. Transitions to familiar people in familiar settings easily; still cautious about unfamiliar settings or new experiences.		c. Transitions to most settings without distress; when distress occurs, can be comforted or redirected.
T4	a. Separation anxiety begins to resolve; is able to make transitions to familiar settings with familiar adults without experiencing distress. When distress occurs, it resolves when the child gets interested in the new setting and playmates.	b. Stranger anxiety emerges. Fear of strangers and new situations causes proximity-seeking behavior such as getting close to primary caregiver, clinging, crying, resistance to social overtures (e.g, hiding behind adult, hiding face).		c. Stranger anxiety begins resolving; may continue to be cautious, but will accept interactions from strangers after watching or observing for a moment. Takes cues (looks to them, watches their reactions) about new situations from familiar adults.
T5	a. Prefers predictable routines and schedule; manages changes in schedule fairly well at the time but may experience problems later.	b. Ritualistic about routines and schedule—likes routines predictably "just so"; exhibits ritualistic behavior around routines; likes routines the same way every time; needs warnings of anticipated transitions and still may resist them; melts down or tantrums when schedule is changed without reminders and preparation.		c. Adapts to changes in schedule when prepared in advance; abrupt or unplanned schedule changes still present problems; adapts more readily in familiar settings except when tired, hungry, or ill.
T6	a. Tries new food when presented; has strong food preferences.	b. Resists new foods on some days and not on others; reduces intake; may become a picky eater or refuse to try new foods when offered.	c. Has small selection of food preferences; still resists new food when presented; eats well on some days and not on others.	d. Food intake and preferences even out; will try new food after many presentations; needs encouragement to try new foods.
T7	a. Develops a sense of property rights; hoards toys and favorite objects.	b. Considers objects being played with as personal property.		c. Recognizes mine and not mine.

Toddler (18-36 months) Assessment

Task: Making Friends

	18-24 months	24-30 months	30-36 months
MF1	a. Calms self with verbal support from adults and transitional objects.	b. Calms self with verbal support from adults; may look for transitional objects to help with the calm-down process after verbal support is provided. Frequency of emotional outburst begins to diminish.	c. Calms self with only verbal support. Use of transitional objects begins to decline except at bedtime and when recovering from intense emotional outbursts.
MF2	a Goes to mirror to look at self; makes faces and shows emotions such as laughing, crying, and so on.	b. Calls own name when looking at photographs or in the mirror.	c. Calls names of friends in photographs or in the mirror.
MF3	a. Develops preferences for types of play and types of toys.	b. Develops play themes that are repeated again and again (such as mommy or firefighter).	c. Begins exploration of a wider range of play themes. Themes often come from new experiences.
MF4	a. Perfects gross motor skills such as running, climbing, and riding push toys. Fine motor skills with manipulatives (simple puzzles, Duplos, and so on) are emerging.	b. Likes physical challenges such as running fast, jumping high, and going up and down stairs. Plays with preferred manipulatives for increasing periods of time.	c. Competently exhibits a wide range of physical skills. Begins to be interested in practicing skills such as throwing a ball, riding a tricycle, or completing a puzzle.
MF5	a. Play may be onlooker, solitary, or parallel in nature.	b. Play is predominantly parallel in nature.	c. Exhibits associative play with familiar play partners.
MF6	a. Exhibits symbolic play.	b. Practices and explores a wide variety of symbolic play themes and roles.	
MF7	a. Objects to strangers' presence; clings, cries, and seeks support when strangers are around.	b. Objection to strangers begins to diminish; may still be wary of strangers or new situations.	c. Is able to venture into strange or new situations if prepared in advance and supported by adults.
MF8	a. Uses single words to indicate needs and wants such as "muk" for "I want milk," or "bye bye" for "Let's go bye bye."	b. Uses phrases and 2- to 3-word sentences to indicate needs and wants.	c. Uses 4- to 6-word sentences to indicate needs and wants.
MF9	a. Connects emotions with behaviors; uses language to express these connections.	b. Uses emotional ideas in play. / c. Elaborates on emotional ideas and understanding to play with objects.	d. Begins emotional thinking; begins to understand emotional cause-and-effect relationships.
MF10	a. Takes turns with toys and materials with adult support and facilitation.	b. Takes turns with toys and materials with friend, sometimes without adult support.	
MF11	a. Experiments with behavior that accomplishes a goal; may bite, pinch, poke, scratch, push, and so on while trying to make things happen.	b. Begins to anticipate what might happen when actions are taken; chooses to make things happen if outcomes are desirable (e.g., trade toys with a friend who will stay and play), and resists action if outcomes are undesirable (e.g., teacher putting markers away if child chews on the tips).	

Toddler (18-36 months) Assessment

Task: Exploring Roles

	18-24 months	**24-30 months**	**30-36 months**
ER1	a. Explores roles related to self and family.	b. Explores roles related to self, friends, family, and neighborhood.	c. Explores roles related to self, friends, family, neighborhood, and the community at large.
ER2	a. Is unable to choose or modify behavior in response to physical or social cues of situations; persists in using behavior that doesn't work in situations.	b. Begins to choose or modify behavior in response to physical and social cues of situations; when one behavior isn't working, may stop and try something else.	c. Chooses and modifies behavior in response to the physical and social cues of a situation; tries to choose the behaviors that will get what he or she wants; can change behaviors if they are not working.
ER3	a. Does not understand the impact of own behavior on others.	b. Begins to understand the impact of own behavior on others; shows interest and awareness of the emotional behaviors of friends and others.	c. Understands the impact of own behavior on others; anticipates how friends or others will react.
ER4	a. Uses props to play roles; becomes the occupant of the role (e.g., is superman when wearing a cape or mommy when holding a baby). Prefers familiar roles.	b. Uses props to adopt roles; abandons roles when the props are removed; changes between familiar and favorite roles in dramatic play.	c. Can play roles with or without props. Transitions between roles frequently and easily (e.g., can be the mommy, then the daddy, then the monster during same play period).

Toddler (18-36 months) Assessment

Task: Communicating with Parents, Teachers, and Friends

	18-24 months		24-30 months	30-36 months
CM1	a. Expressive vocabulary increases; uses about 200 words on a regular basis. Expressive language continues to be telegraphic, where single words may carry expanded meaning only understood by familiar caregivers.		b. Vocabulary size begins to grow rapidly; sentence length begins to increase with 3 or 4 words in some sentences.	c. Sentence length continues to grow. Four- to six-word sentences predominate expressive language. Vocabulary continues to expand; expressive vocabulary is adequate to make most needs and wants understood by others.
CM2	a. Uses a greater variety of sounds and sound combinations, simplifying the word if it is too complex (such as pane for plane, tephone for telephone); enjoys experimenting with inflection that sounds like adult speech although it is not yet understandable.		b. Rapid development of new sound combinations and new words that are understandable to adults. Uses language functionally—to ask for things and get needs met and to interact with friends.	c. Is able to use language to get most needs and wants met by familiar caregivers and to interact with friends.
CM3	a. Seeks vocal interactions with familiar people; can communicate needs and wants to familiar caregivers; begins to be wary of talking to strangers.		b. Resists interactions with strangers; hides, withdraws, or objects to encouragement to talk to strangers.	
CM4	a. 20-25% of language is intelligible to strangers. Parents and caregivers can understand more.		b. 60-65% of language is intelligible to strangers. Parents and caregivers understand most of the child's expressive language.	
CM5	a. "Reads" book from front to back; turns books right side up to look at them.	b. Makes sounds that connect to pictures in books.	c. Listens to a complete story from beginning to end; asks to read familiar books over and over again.	d. Likes to look at books independently; "reads" books to self.
CM6	a. Actively experiments with the environment; follows visual displacement of objects.		b. Begins transition to symbolic thought. Uses formed mental images to solve problems. Thought processes relate to concrete experiences and objects.	c. Begins transition to pre-operational stage characterized by the beginning of symbolic thought and the use of mental images and words.

Toddler (18-36 months) Assessment

Task: Problem-solving

	18-24 months	24-30 months	30-36 months
PS1	a. Interest in toileting is limited to watching; may show interest in flushing toilet, sitting on the toilet, or washing hands. Interest may wax and wane quickly.	b. Toilet play stage of toileting; interested in playing at toileting activities such as taking off diaper, sitting on the toilet, using toilet paper, flushing the toilet, and washing hands.	c. Toilet practice begins; likes to repeat toileting activities again and again, with or without success.
PS2	a. Activity level increases; requests and seeks out motor activities. Does not control activity level without adult support; yet resists adult support in modulating activity level.	b. Activity level continues to increase; continues to seek out motor activities. Begins to modulate activity levels with verbal and physical adult support (e.g., slow down, take a deep breath).	c. Alternates between high levels of activity and periods of calm, quieter activity. Can modulate activity level with verbal reminders from adults.
PS3	a. On-task behavior begins to increase.	b. Able to sustain favorite activities for increasingly longer periods of time; extends on-task play time at favorite activities to 10 minutes. Still loses interest in other activities quickly.	c. Stays on task at favorite manipulative activities for sustained periods of time; extends on-task play time at favorite activities to 20 minutes. Still loses interest in other activities quickly.
PS4	a. Carries toys around from place to place. b. Undresses; takes off shoes, socks, and clothes. c. Turns door knob to open door.	d. Holds cup with one hand to drink. e. Shows preference for one hand.	f. Unzips zipper. g. Pulls pants up. h. Zips zipper.
PS5	a. Propels riding toys with feet. b. Runs; collapses to stop forward movement.	c. Goes up stairs without alternating feet, holding on to handrail. d. Runs; begins to control starting and stopping. e. Balances on one foot.	f. Goes up stairs alternating feet, holding on to handrail. g. Jumps up and down on two feet. h. Pedals tricycle.

Toddler (18-36 months) Assessment

Task: Expressing Feelings with Parents, Teachers, and Friends

	18-24 months		24-30 months	30-36 months	
E1	a. Begins to create mental images of emotional behaviors.	b. Uses behavior to express emotions (e.g., stomps foot).	c. Distinguishes between emotions and the behaviors that go with that emotion (e.g., feeling mad vs. acting mad).	d. Understands how one feeling relates to another (e.g., being disappointed about getting a toy and getting angry as a result of the disappointment).	
E2	a. Emotional intensity is not regulated—minor and major events get similar reactions; falls apart easily.		b. Begins to regulate emotional intensity in some situations; falls apart less frequently.	c. Regulates emotional intensity most of the time; seldom falls apart.	d. Figures out how to respond with appropriate emotions to most situations.
E3	a. Watches and remembers emotional behaviors exhibited by others; uses observations in future interactions.		b. Puts emotional mental images to work in pretend play; can make-believe or pretend to be angry, happy, sad, and so on.		
E4	a. Knows rules that have been reinforced consistently but still needs reminders and physical adult support to comply.		b. Follows rules that have been reinforced consistently with verbal reminders and physical adult support.	c. Follows rules that have been reinforced consistently with just verbal reminders.	
E5	a. Unable to label own feelings.		b. Can label some feelings; uses the same feeling to represent many feelings (e.g., mad for angry, frustrated, irritated, unhappy, etc.).	c. Labels most of his or her own feelings; can differentiate between similar emotions and label them appropriately.	
E6	a. Unable to understand how others feel.		b. Begins to understand how others feel when observing others but not when he or she is a part of the interaction.	c. Understands how others feel when the behavior exhibited is consistent with the emotion being felt (e.g., angry child is yelling, stomping foot, saying, "No!").	
E7	a. Has difficulty delaying gratification.		b. Can delay gratification for a short time when supported by adults.	c. Can delay gratification for a few minutes in most situations.	
E8	a. Does not separate fantasy from reality.		b. Can switch from reality to fantasy.	c. Understands "real" and "not real."	
E9	a. Ambivalent about being autonomous; wants to sometimes and doesn't want to at other times.		b. Independent behaviors are increasing; dependent behaviors are decreasing.	c. Independent behaviors are usually present.	
E10	a. Has little control over impulses.		b. Controls impulses in some situations or with support from adults.	c. Most impulses are under control.	
E11	a. Loses emotional control often and intensely.		b. Loss of emotional control is less frequent, less intense, and less prolonged.	c. Infrequently loses emotional control.	

Toddler (18-36 months) Observation and Assessment Summary

	18-24 months		24-30 months		30-36 months	
	Subtask	Date	Subtask	Date	Subtask	Date
Task 1 **Transitioning to School**	T1a		T1b		T1c	
	T2a		T2b		T2c	
	T3a		T3b		T3c	
	T4a		T4b		T4c	
	T5a		T5b		T5c	
	T6a		T6b		T6d	
			T6c			
	T7a		T7b		T7c	
Task 2 **Making Friends**	MF1a		MF1b		MF1c	
	MF2a		MF2b		MF2c	
	MF3a		MF3b		MF3c	
	MF4a		MF4b		MF4c	
	MF5a		MF5b		MF5c	
	MF6a		MF6b		MF6b	
	MF7a		MF7b		MF7c	
	MF8a		MF8b		MF8c	
	MF9a		MF9b		MF9d	
			MF9c			
	MF10a		MF10b		MF10b	
	MF11a		MF11b		MF11b	
Task 3 **Exploring Roles**	ER1a		ER1b		ER1c	
	ER2a		ER2b		ER2c	
	ER3a		ER3b		ER3c	
	ER4a		ER4b		ER4c	
Task 4 **Communicating with Parents, Teachers, and Friends**	CM1a		CM1b		CM1c	
	CM2a		CM2b		CM2c	
	CM3a		CM3b		CM3b	
	CM4a		CM4b		CM4b	
	CM5a		CM5c		CM5d	
	CM5b					
	CM6a		CM6b		CM6c	

	18-24 months		24-30 months		30-36 months	
	Subtask	Date	Subtask	Date	Subtask	Date
Task 5 **Problem-solving**	PS1a		PS1b		PS1c	
	PS2a		PS2b		PS2c	
	PS3a		PS3b		PS3c	
	PS4a		PS4d		PS4f	
	PS4b		PS4e		PS4g	
	PS4c				PS4h	
	PS5a		PS5c		PS5f	
	PS5b		PS5d		PS5g	
			PS5e		PS5h	
Task 6 **Expressing Feelings** **with Parents,** **Teachers, and Friends**	E1a		E1c		E1d	
	E1b					
	E2a		E2b		E2c	
					E2d	
	E3a		E3b		E3b	
	E4a		E4b		E4c	
	E5a		E5b		E5c	
	E6a		E6b		E6c	
	E7a		E7b		E7c	
	E8a		E8b		E8c	
	E9a		E9b		E9c	
	E10a		E10b		E10c	
	E11a		E11b		E11c	

Concepts Learned in Me and My Body

I can recognize myself in a mirror.

I can play interactive games.

I can play near another child.

I can point to named body parts (eyes, ears, nose, mouth, chin, elbow, arm, knee, ankle, wrist, and so on).

I can name body parts.

Eyes are for seeing.

Noses are for smelling.

Mouths are for eating.

Ears are for hearing.

I can play chase.

I can climb two- or three-step stairs.

I can roll a ball.

I can turn the pages of a book.

I can ride a small riding toy without pedals.

I can jump in place.

I can hop on one foot.

I can walk with balance.

I can walk on tiptoes.

I can match pictures.

I can name pictured items.

I can use glue sticks and art materials to create a project.

I can follow one-step and two-step directions.

I can take things off.

I can put things on.

Conference Summary Form

Child's name _____

Parent/Teacher Conference Summary Form	
Formal Conferences with Written Documentation	Date: Who attended: Date: Who attended: Date: Who attended: Date: Who attended:
Informal Conferences/Written	Date: With whom: Date: With whom: Date: With whom: Date: With whom:
Formal Oral Conferences	Date: With whom: Date: With whom: Date: With whom:
Informal Oral Conferences	Date: With whom: Date: With whom: Date: With whom:
Telephone Conferences	Date: With whom: Date: With whom: Date: With whom:

Cover Sheet

Innovations

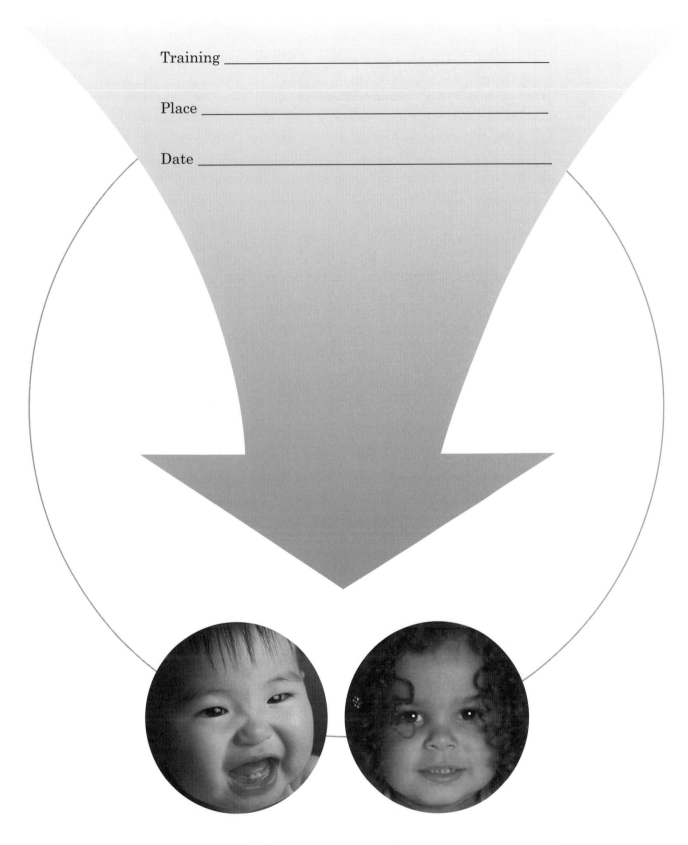

Training _____

Place _____

Date _____

Creating Environments for Young Children

Every classroom has an unusual "extra" teacher, and that teacher is the environment. Children learn through the active exploration of their surroundings, so teachers must plan an appropriate learning environment for the children in their care. Children in full-day programs have to "live" in their school settings (Greenman, 1988). Because of this, stimulation activities must be balanced across the important dimensions of activity (quiet or active), location (indoor or outdoor), and initiator (child-initiated or adult-initiated) (Bredekamp, Copple 1997; National Academy of Early Childhood Programs, 1991). Teachers must include items from *Innovations* in Environment on the possibilities plan to add to the environment.

Teachers have the following responsibilities for the environment:

▶ *Creating the Environment*—Teachers use their knowledge of what a classroom needs to determine room arrangement and the organization of materials.

▶ *Maintaining the Environment*—Teachers keep the environment safe by inspecting toys and classroom for problems. Broken toys or toys with missing pieces are fixed or discarded. Toys and surfaces are routinely disinfected.

▶ *Refreshing the Environment*—Teachers plan for different experiences by adding a variety of different materials and taking away some of the old materials. A balance between novel toys, materials, and experiences and familiar toys, materials, and experiences is achieved.

Bredekamp, C. & C. Copple (1997). *Developmentally appropriate practice in early childhood programs*, Revised edition. Washington, DC: National Association for the Education of Young Children (NAEYC).
Greenman, J. (1988). *Caring spaces, learning places: Children's environments that work*. Redmond, WA: Exchange Press.
National Academy of Early Childhood Programs. (1991). *Accreditation criteria and procedures*. Washington, DC: National Academy of Early Childhood Programs.

Creating Environments for Young Children—Classroom Checklist

Use the following checklist to evaluate your classroom. Place a check to indicate if you agree, somewhat agree, or disagree.

	Agree	Somewhat Agree	Disagree
1. Elements are in place that create a sense of calm in the classroom.	☐	☐	☐
2. Sufficient soft elements and nooks help make the environment more home-like.	☐	☐	☐
3. Appropriate places are provided for children's things in the classroom.	☐	☐	☐
4. Classroom is a predictable environment that includes both novel and interesting features.	☐	☐	☐
5. Classroom includes places to be alone (meltdown) that do not sacrifice visual supervision.	☐	☐	☐
6. Classroom includes opportunities for different perspectives (platform, windows, doors).	☐	☐	☐
7. Classroom includes places to climb.	☐	☐	☐
8. Materials and toys are stored on low shelves in clear, labeled containers.	☐	☐	☐
9. Stimulation in the classroom can be decreased and increased (light, music, nature sounds).	☐	☐	☐
10. The classroom and the materials are safe and appropriate.	☐	☐	☐

Use this evaluation to determine a goal for improving your classroom. Write it here. (For example, create places for each child to put his or her things; or add some soft elements, such as pillows or carpets, to the environment.)

My goal for my classroom is:

Curriculum Planning Process

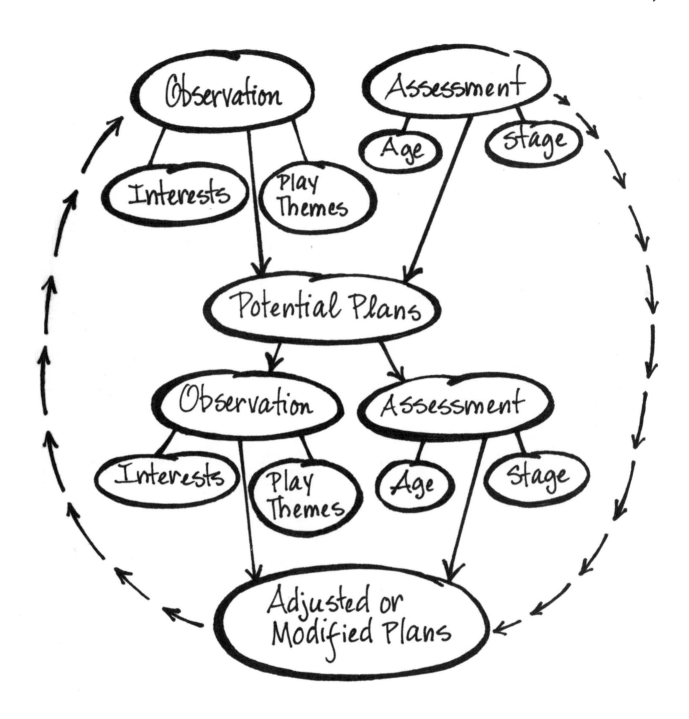

Gardner's Multiple Intelligences

INNOVATIONS

Intelligence	Description
Linguistic	Sensitivity to the meaning and order of words
Logico-mathematical	Ability to handle chains of reasoning and recognize patterns and order
Musical	Sensitivity to pitch, melody, rhythm, and tone
Bodily-kinesthetic	Ability to use the body skillfully and handle objects adroitly
Spatial	Ability to perceive the world accurately and to recreate or transform aspects of that world
Naturalist	Ability to recognize and classify the numerous species of an environment
Interpersonal	Ability to understand people and relationships
Intrapersonal (also called emotional intelligence by Goleman)	Access to one's emotional life as a means to understand oneself and others.

All of the multiple intelligences begin at birth. Early indicators of different intelligences can be seen in children in many ways. Some children are watchers—they like to watch others try new things. Others are doers—they have to be in the middle of any experience embracing it all. Still others listen carefully to what goes on around them before they begin to interact. These differences emerge from the individual's unique collection of intelligences and are part of what makes each of us different from one another.

The theory of multiple intelligences offers teachers a wonderful framework for interacting with and teaching children. It is very freeing for teachers to know that it is acceptable to treat children differently—when the treatment matches the child's learning style.

Icebreakers

Purpose of Icebreakers

Icebreakers help participants learn about each other and the workshop in general. If the participants already know each other, an icebreaker may not be necessary. However, even when participants know each other, an icebreaker may provide an emotional connection or a way for them to get to know each other better. Try the following icebreakers to help your participants get started!

Baby Pictures

Collect photos of the participants when they were children and display them on a bulletin board. Number the photographs and ask the participants to identify the younger versions of the people present.

Nametag Grouping

Before the participants arrive, prepare nametags. Use a variety of stickers to group participants. For example, use stickers with pictures of different animals (bears, turtles, birds, cats) and arrange seating at different tables labeled with the animal names. When the participants arrive, ask them to sit at the table that matches their nametag. At the table, ask the participants to introduce themselves and identify one question they would like answered at the workshop. Ask the group leaders to present these questions while someone records them on a chart or overhead transparency. Use the questions to guide your presentation, and make sure to answer the questions in your summary.

Longest to Shortest

As participants arrive, give each person a handout with the following questions:

I have taught _____ years.

I have been married _____ years.

I have been driving _____ years.

It takes me _____ minutes to drive (travel) to work.

My oldest child (grandchild) is _____.

My youngest child (grandchild) is _____.

Icebreakers (continued)

When the participants have completed the survey, ask them to go to the back or front of the room. Arrange the participants according to their answers, such as longest to shortest, oldest to youngest, and so on. Award prizes for participants who have taught the longest and the shortest amount of time.

I Feel Like a ...

Ask the participants to write the name of the animal they most feel like today. Ask them to share what they wrote with the other participants at their table (or their row, and so on) and explain why that particular animal is a reflection of how they feel.

Purse Scavenger Hunt

Before the participants arrive, make a list of common or unusual items that individuals might have in their pockets or purse (for example, clippers, newspaper, bill, screwdriver, key chain, vacation souvenir, book, phone numbers, pen, crayons, safety pin, diaper, candy, mints, tissue, mirror, photo of pet, grocery coupons, inspirational book, bookmark, passport, sandwich, bird seed). Call out one item, and the participants who have that item in their pocket or purse race to the front of the room. Provide small prizes to winners.

I Can/I Can't

Ask the participants to turn to their nearest neighbor and tell her or him something they do really well (for example, cooking, singing, peeling apples, driving, or budgeting). Switch so that everyone gets a turn. Next ask the participants to turn to their nearest neighbor and tell her or him something they cannot do very well (for example, cooking, handwriting, or playing cards). Switch again. Ask for some common answers. Who is a great cook? Who really needs some help cooking? Suggest that these people meet at the break, and so on.

My Best Day Teaching

As the participants arrive, hand out blank sheets of paper and pens. Ask the participants to write about their best day teaching. Choose some interesting ones to share out loud.

Icebreakers

Gossip

Play this variation of gossip. Whisper to someone in the front row, "Break will be at 10:00" (or whatever time fits). Ask the person to whisper the message to the next person and so on all around the room. Ask the last person to give the announcement to the whole group.

Visualization

Research has shown that people who can visualize success are more likely to be successful. Ask the participants to visualize a great day teaching. Brainstorm and write some common elements on a chart.

Vacation Dreaming

Ask the participants to remember their most relaxing or exciting moment on vacation. Talk about how remembering a pleasant experience can help us to survive a stressful one.

Infant Developmental Tasks

(Birth to 18 months)

Separating from Parents

Connecting with School and Teacher

Relating to Self and Others

Communicating with Parents, Teachers, and Friends

Moving Around

Expressing Feelings with Parents, Teachers, and Friends

Infant/Toddler Temperament Chart

Temperament Chart

Nine character traits have been identified to gauge a child's temperament and to help determine the most effective method of caring for each child:

1) activity level
2) regularity of biological rhythms (sleeping, eating, and elimination)
3) approach/withdrawal tendencies
4) mood, positive to negative
5) intensity of reaction
6) adaptability
7) sensitivity to light, touch, taste, sound, and sights
8) distractibility, and
9) persistence

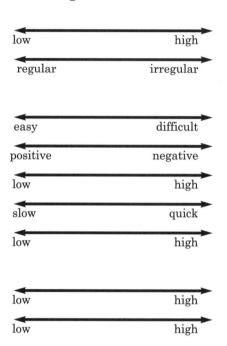

Interactive Experiences Checklist

When teachers plan interactive experiences such as the ones that follow, children's self-concepts will have opportunities to flourish.

- ☐ Support children's feelings of belonging. Make it clear that all children belong in your classroom.
- ☐ Provide understandable and consistent limits.
- ☐ Use encouragement (instead of praise) to describe completed tasks and recognize effort.
- ☐ Validate children's uniqueness, focusing on your positive feelings about their unique qualities.
- ☐ Give children opportunities to have your undivided, personal attention regularly.
- ☐ Provide lots of opportunities for choice.
- ☐ Provide opportunities for exploration, investigation, and development of new alternatives.
- ☐ Let children know that you believe they can succeed.
- ☐ Encourage children to make and keep their own rules.
- ☐ Make sure interactions are characterized by mutual respect.
- ☐ Help children handle failure by being close and recognizing their effort.
- ☐ Help children persist.
- ☐ Help children cooperate and work together to accomplish things.
- ☐ Be an ally to help identify potential solutions to solving problems.
- ☐ Accept children's solutions to their own problems.
- ☐ Prevent frustration that comes from unrealistic expectations.

Language Behaviors Checklist

Infants

AGE	LANGUAGE BEHAVIORS
BIRTH-6 MONTHS	• Responds to familiar voices. • Changes cry with emotional state. • Turns eyes and head toward the source of sound. • Is aware of the sounds he makes. • Makes soft vowel sounds: uh, ah.
7-10 MONTHS	• Turns head and shoulders toward soft, familiar sounds. • Imitates intonational patterns of familiar phrases using some vowel and consonant patterns. • Practices a variety of intonational and inflectional patterns. • Understands simple phrases such as bye-bye, no-no, and his own name. • Directs vocalizations toward people and familiar objects in the environment.
11-16 MONTHS	• Says first words, da-da, ma-ma, muk (milk), etc. • Uses several words correctly and consistently. • Points or looks to familiar objects when asked to do so. • Imitates and jabbers in response to human voice. • Frowns when scolded. • Imitates sounds he hears: moo, baa baa, etc. • Expresses bodily needs with nonverbal and verbal responses.
16-18 MONTHS	• Begins to identify body parts; is able to point to eyes and nose. • Uses several meaningful words that may not be articulated correctly such as ba-ba for bottle, muk for milk, etc. • May use one word to represent several things, including wa-wa for I want water, look at the water, and I spilled the water.

Language Behaviors Checklist

Toddlers

INNOVATIONS

AGE	LANGUAGE BEHAVIORS
18-24 MONTHS	• Follows simple commands without visual clues. • Enjoys books; likes being read to if book is familiar; will ask to have the same book read again and again. • Points to familiar pictures in books or magazines. • Develops a sense of "me" and "mine." • Uses a variety of common words consistently heard in the classroom or at home (usually between 10-20 words). • Refers to self by name. • Puts familiar words together to make simple sentences such as "Daddy work" or "Mommy bye-bye" and "all gone." • Talks mainly about self. • Imitates animal or object sounds. • Expresses refusal by saying "no."
24-30 MONTHS	• Likes listening to music or singing. • Sings short songs or says short fingerplays. • Imitates 3- to 4-word sentences. • Reacts to sound by telling what is heard or running to look at the source of the sound. • Continues to express refusal by saying "no." • Objects to help from others; wants to do it all by himself.
30-36 MONTHS	• Understands and uses simple verbs. • Understands pronouns, prepositions, adverbs, and adjectives such as "in," "me," "big," "go," "more," and so on. • Uses plurals. • Understands contrasts such as yes/no, come/go, run/stop, hot/cold. • Uses complete sentences frequently. • Answers simple questions from familiar people. • Uses "I" and "me."

Note to Parents

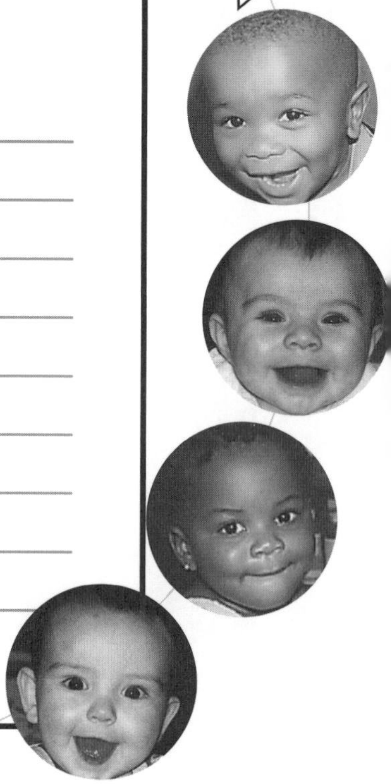

_____

_____

_____

_____

_____

_____

_____

_____

_____

Note to Parents

_____

_____

_____

_____

_____

_____

_____

_____

_____

Observation/Assessment Instrument—Helpful Hints for Completing

▶ Plan to observe regularly, but don't overlook daily observations that occur in real time. If you note a new skill, a play interest, or an emotional response, write it on the Communication Sheet so you won't forget it, and attach a copy to the assessment. Use these "real-time" observations to support formal observations.

▶ Take anecdotal notes as you observe. Notes can be about one child, or about more than one child. If you record information about more than one child, copy the note and file it in both children's files.

▶ After taking anecdotal notes, look at the appropriate assessment to determine if you observed any of the assessment items listed. If you did, simply date the assessment item, indicating that you have an anecdotal note that documents your observation of the skill (i.e., Anecdotal Note, 3/3/00 or AN 3/3/00).

▶ If you don't observe an item during the time range of the assessment, and subsequent skills are noted, put "Not Observed" or "N/O" in the date space.

▶ Put the date ranges for the child on the chart below the age ranges to cue you to the child's birth date and confirm you are observing the right sections.

▶ Look for secondary sources for some assessment items. For example, check Communication Sheets, Books Read Lists, word lists, anecdotal records, and any other sources to see if you can confirm the presence of skills from these sources. For example, "word list" to support CM6c or "Communication Sheet" for S4c.

Observation/Assessment Instrument, Infant (0-18 months)

Task: Relating to Self and Others

	0-6 months	6-12 months		12-18 months
R1	a. Calms self with adult support.	b. Calms self with support from adults and/or transitional objects.		c. Calms self with transitional objects.
R2	a. Unaware of own image in mirror.	b. Curious about own image in mirrors and photographs.	c. Discovers self in mirror and photographs.	d. Differentiates own image from images of others.
R3	a. Begins to demonstrate preferences for different types of sensory stimuli.	b. Prefers some types of stimuli to others.		c. Is interested in pursuing favorite stimulation activities again and again.
R4	a. Develops a multi-sensory interest in the world—wants to see, touch, mouth, hear, and hold objects.	b. Uses senses to explore and discover the near environment.		c. Uses motor movements to enhance sensory exploration of the environment.
R5	a. Play is predominantly unoccupied in nature.	b. Play is predominantly onlooker in nature.	c. Play is predominantly solitary in nature.	
R6	a. Exhibits practice play.			b. Exhibits symbolic play.
R7	a. Develops an interest in the human world.	b. Seeks interactions with responsive adults; interested also in what other children are doing.	c. Seeks most interactions with familiar adults; fascinated by what other children are doing.	d. Prefers interactions with familiar adults; resists interaction with unfamiliar adults; may be cautious with unfamiliar friends.
R8	a. Does not distinguish between needs (social interaction, a new position, holding instead of lying in the bed) and wants (food, diaper changes, sleep).	b. Begins to distinguish between needs and wants; can communicate differently about different needs and wants.	c. Uses objects, gestures, and behaviors to indicate needs and wants.	d. Uses single words to indicate needs and wants like "muk" for "I want milk," or "bye-bye" for "Let's go bye-bye."
R9	a. Creates mental images of emotions and emotional responses to situations.			b. Begins to understand how feelings relate to others.
R10	a. Unable to negotiate interactions with peers without direct adult support and facilitation.	b. Calls for help loudly by crying or screaming when problems occur during exploration of the environment or with peers.	c. Exchanges or trades with peers to get a desired toy or material with direct adult support and facilitation.	d. Asks other children to walk away when conflict arises between children; expects the other child to do so.
R11	a. Explores environment and the things in it orally. May bite, poke, scratch, or pinch others during exploration.			b. Experiments with behavior that gets a reaction; may bite, pinch, poke, scratch during interactions with others to see what happens.

One-day Training Agenda

7:45   Registration

8:00   Welcome, Overview of Day, and Introductions

9:00   Developmental Tasks

9:30   Observation and Assessment
        Correlate to Planning Form
        Anecdotal Records

10:00   Break

10:15   Child Development and Classroom Challenges

10:45   Interactive Experiences

11:00   Teaching
        Teacher Competencies
        Parent Partnerships
        Communication Sheet

11:30   Environments

12:00   Lunch

1:00   Activities and Experiences

1:00   Webbing

2:15   Planning Pages

2:30   Possibilities

3:00   Concepts Learned, Resources

3:30   Break

3:45   Forms and Other Means of Communication

4:45   Summary, Closing, and Evaluation

Parent Visit Log

School Name _____

Date	Name of Parent
1. _____	
2. _____	
3. _____	
4. _____	
5. _____	
6. _____	
7. _____	
8. _____	
9. _____	
10. _____	
11. _____	
12. _____	
13. _____	
14. _____	
15. _____	
16. _____	
17. _____	
18. _____	
19. _____	
20. _____	
21. _____	
22. _____	
23. _____	
24. _____	
25. _____	
26. _____	
27. _____	
28. _____	
29. _____	
30. _____	

Parten Types of Play Chart

Types of Peer Play	Definitions	Examples	How to Support
1. Unoccupied Play	Children watch others at play.		
2. Onlooker Play	Children watch others at play, but seek to be near them and may respond.		
3. Solitary Independent Play	Children play alone with objects without interacting with others.		
4. Parallel Activity	Children play alongside each other with similar toys, but do not interact.		
5. Associative Play	Children participate in activities with others, but specific goals or roles are not assigned.		
6. Cooperative Play	Children cooperate with each other to create play situations with defined roles and goals.		

Parten Types of Play Chart

PIES

Physical Intellectual* Emotional Social

*Includes Language and Cognition

Ping-ponging

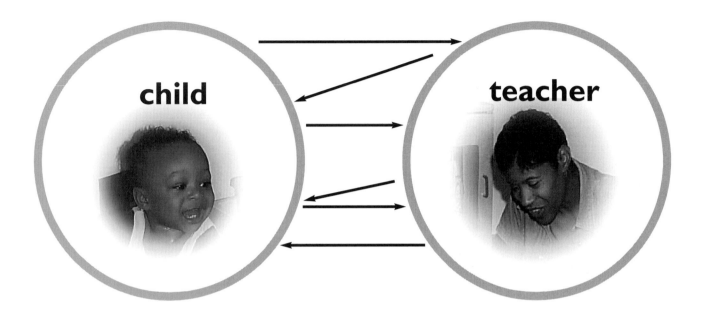

The teacher is not "doing something" to the child or trying to get the child to do a particular thing. Instead, the interaction is a gentle interchange between adult and child—two equals.

Play Theorist Summary

Piaget and Play

Three Types of Play Behavior

1. Practice Play—(ages birth to 2 years) repetitions of the same movements and actions, both with or without objects
2. Symbolic Play—(ages 2 to 7 years) the beginning of traditional dramatic play where children recreate in play what they are seeing in the real world
3. Play-with-rules—(ages 7 to 12 years) where children begin to impose rules to govern play or to manipulate interactions

Parten and Play

Six Types of Peer Play

1. Unoccupied Play—Children watch others at play.
2. Onlooker Play—Children watch others at play, but seek to be near them and may respond to the play of others.
3. Solitary Independent Play—Children play alone with objects without interacting with others, regardless of how near.
4. Parallel Activity—Children play alongside each other with similar toys— beside each other rather than with each other.
5. Associative Play—Activities occur between children although no specific roles are assigned or play goal identified.
6. Cooperative Play—Children cooperate with others to create play situations.

Vygotsky and Play

▶ Children socially construct what they know in the context of their family and cultural experiences.

▶ Zone of Proximal Development (ZPD)—the range of tasks a child cannot yet handle alone, but can accomplish with the help of adults and more skilled peers.

▶ Engaging in joint play with children helps them develop skills that they can later use in social play with peers.

Portfolio Planning Form

Suggestions of Items for Children's Portfolios:

▶ Samples of children's work (drawings with different media such as crayons, watercolors, markers, brushes, etc., collages, self-portraits, etc.)

▶ Photographs

▶ Assessment Summary

▶ Parent Conference Summary

▶ Anecdotal Records/Observations

▶ Audio Tapes, Videotapes

▶ Books Read Lists

▶ Vocabulary Lists

▶ Concepts Learned Lists

▶ Selected Communication Sheets (with significant events or important notes from parents to teachers or from teachers to parents)

▶ Accident/Incident Reports

▶ Parent Visit Log

▶ Copies of Favorite Fingerplays and Songs

Possibilities

Parent Possibilities

Teacher-Initiated

Parent Participation

Innovations in Environments

Observation/Assessment Possibilities

Interactive Experiences

Plan

Web

Dramatic Possibilities

Art/Sensory Possibilities

Curiosity Possibilities

Music Possibilities

Movement Possibilities

Literacy Possibilities

Outdoor Possibilities

Project Possibilities

Books	**Picture File Pictures/Vocabulary**

Rhymes & Fingerplays	**Music/Songs**	**Prop Boxes**

Possibilities

Parent Possibilities

Teacher-Initiated Parent Picture book

Parent Participation

Innovations in Environments

Rattles
Mirrors
Empty bath items
Sleep items

Observation/Assessment Possibilities

Tameka= S1c, S2b, S3b, S4c, S5b, S6b, S7b
Joseph= S1c, S2b, S3b, S4c, S5b, S6b, S7b
Trevarious= S1c, S2b, S3b, S4c, S5b, S6b, S7b
Sue= S1c, S2b, S3b, S4c, S5b, S6b, S7b

Interactive Experiences

leave a written record for other teachers
use routines for interaction and learning
provide physical and visual support for new
experiences

Plan (Completed)

Web

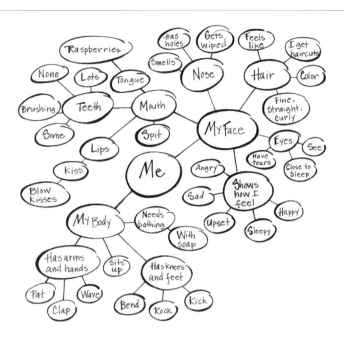

Dramatic Possibilities   Bathing Baby 62, Taking Things Off 62

Art/Sensory Possibilities   Drawing 63, Foot Painting 64

Curiosity Possibilities   Peek-a-boo 64, Mirror Play 64

Music Possibilities   Johnny Works with One Hammer 68

Movement Possibilities   Johnny Junper 69

Literacy Possibilities   Parent Picture Book 65, On the Day I was Born 66

Outdoor Possibilities   View from a Blanket 70, Outside Doll Baths 70

Project Possibilities   Repeated Foot Painting 71

Books	Picture File Pictures/Vocabulary	
On the Day I was Born by Debi Chocolate From Head to Toe by Eric Carle	Babies Eyes Faces Noses	Babies Outside Hands Mouths Ears

Rhymes & Fingerplays	Music/Songs	Prop Boxes
Eye Winker, Tom Tinker	Johnny Works with One Hammer	Things That Go On My Head Things That Go On My Hands

Problem-solving Worksheet

1. Clearly defined problem/issue

2. Research problem/issue

3. Brainstorm solutions

4. Specific action plan

5. Plan for follow-up

Project Worksheet

Teacher Name _____

Projects are repeated activities or experiences that stretch over a period of time, instead of activities that take place in a short amount of time in one day. Projects are important because they provide continuity of experience, as well as an opportunity for children to practice, perfect, and enjoy an experience again and again. Unlike projects with preschoolers, which often focus on content knowledge and how children interpret this knowledge, projects with infants and toddlers almost always focus on experiences.

Choose an activity appropriate for the children in your classroom.

_____ Page _____

Now reconsider the activity. Explain how you will change the activity into a project that is appropriate for the children in your classroom.

Make the plans necessary to implement the project in your classroom (for example, time of day when it is appropriate, how many days to repeat the project, materials needed, note to parents, and a plan to document).

Prop Box Worksheet

INNOVATIONS

Teacher Name _____

Prop boxes are valuable resources for teachers because they help you collect, organize, and store materials and resources. Start by developing one prop box, and you will be hooked! Storing items in clear plastic containers helps you to quickly identify resources as curriculum emerges in your classroom. Listing prop boxes on the Possibilities Plan you post in your classroom will also remind parents to support the curriculum by collecting these valuable teaching resources.

Prop Box Chosen _____ page_____

Materials List

☐	
☐	
☐	
☐	
☐	
☐	
☐	
☐	
☐	
☐	
☐	
☐	
☐	
☐	

Place a check next to the materials that you already have.

Write a note to parents to ask for additional items.

Before using the prop box in your classroom, ask another teacher to check it for safety. Also, list all materials contained in the prop box on a piece of paper and attach it to the top of the container.

Relationship of Classroom Challenges to Child Development Topics

INNOVATIONS

The following chart shows the relationship of classroom challenges to child development topics.

Classroom Challenges	Child Development Topics
Biting	Encouraging Prosocial Behavior (page 168 in infant book) Handling Biting in the Classroom (page 136 in toddler book)
Aggression	Emotional Development (page 367 in infant book) Managing Normal Aggression in Very Young Children (page 462 in toddler book)
Crying When Mom Leaves	Principles of Developmental Theory (page 34 infant book) Always Say Goodbye (page 62 in toddler book)
Discipline Problems	Physical Development (page 301 in infant book) Handling Temper Tantrums (page 466 in toddler book)

Choose a classroom challenge with which you need help or one in which you are interested. Read the section referenced that explains the appropriate child development topic.

How can knowing about child development help with the classroom challenge you chose?

Release Form

I give permission to _____
to photograph or videotape my child for educational purposes. I agree that I
will receive no compensation or ownership rights to the photographs or
videotapes.

Parent or Guardian _____

Child's Name _____

Date _____

Release Form

I give permission to _____
to photograph or videotape my child for educational purposes. I agree that I
will receive no compensation or ownership rights to the photographs or
videotapes.

Parent or Guardian _____

Child's Name _____

Date _____

Resources for Infant and Toddler Teachers

The American Montessori Society Bulletin
American Montessori Society (AMS)
150 Fifth Avenue
New York, NY 10011

The Black Child Advocate
Black Child Development Institute
1463 Rhode Island Avenue NW
Washington, DC 20001

Child Health Alert
PO Box 388
Newton Highlands, MA 02161

Childhood Education
Association for Childhood Education International (ACEI)
11141 Georgia Avenue, Suite 300
Wheaton, MD 20902

Children and Families
National Head Start Association
1651 Prince Street
Alexandria, VA 22314

Child Welfare
Child Welfare League of America, Inc. (CWLA)
440 First Street NW
Washington, DC 20001

Developmental Psychology
American Psychological Association
1200 Seventeenth Street NW
Washington, DC 20036

Dimensions of Early Childhood
Southern Early Childhood Association
Box 5403 Brady Station
Little Rock, AR 72215

Resources for Infant and Toddler Teachers (continued)

Early Childhood News
PO Box 608
Vandalia, OH 45377

Early Childhood Research Quarterly
National Association for the Education of Young Children
Elsevier Sciences, Ablex Publishing Company
100 Prospect Street
Stamford, CT 06904-0811

Early Childhood Today
Scholastic
Office of Publications
2931 East McCarty Street
PO Box 3710
Jefferson City, MO 65102-3710

Educational Research
American Educational Research Association (AERA)
1230 17th Street NW
Washington, DC 220036

ERIC/EECE Newsletter
805 West Pennsylvania Avenue
Urbana, IL 61801

Exceptional Children
Council for Exceptional Children
1920 Association Drive
Reston, VA 22091

Gifted Child Quarterly
National Association for Gifted Children
4175 Lovell Road, Suite 140
Circle Pines, MN 55014

Head Start Bulletin
USDHHS Head Start
330 C Street NW
Washington, DC 20447

Resources for Infant and Toddler Teachers (continued)

International Association for the Child's Right to Play (IPA)
Dr. Rhonda Clements
Hofstra University
278 Swim Center
Hempstead, NY 11549-1000
or
c/o Mr. Robin C. Moore
North Carolina State University, School of Design
Box 7701
Raleigh, NC 27695-7701

Journal of Research in Early Childhood Education International
11501 Georgia Avenue, Suite 315
Wheaton, MD 20902

Young Children
NAEYC
1509 16th Street NW
Washington, DC 20036-1426

Resources for Trainers

Alexander, N.P. (2000). *Workshops that work!: The essential guide to successful training and workshops*. Beltsville, MD: Gryphon House.

Bloom, P.J. (2000). *Workshop essentials: Planning and presenting dynamic workshops*. Lake Forest, IL: New Horizons.

Jones, E. (1986). *Teaching adults: An active learning approach.* Washington, DC: NAEYC.

Jones, E. (1993). *Growing teachers: Partnerships in staff development*. Washington, DC: NAEYC.

Katz, L.G. (1984). *More talks with teachers.* Urbana, IL: ERIC Clearinghouse on Elementary and Early Childhood Education.

Newstrom, J.W. & E.E. Scannell. (1980). *Games trainers play: Experimental learning exercises*. New York: McGraw/Hill.

Pike, R.W. (1994). *Creative training techniques handbook: Tips, tactics, and how-to's for delivering effective training*. Minneapolis, MN: Lakewoods Books.

Tertell, E.A., S.M. Klein, & J.L. Jewett. (1998). *When teachers reflect: Journeys toward effective, inclusive practice*. Washington, DC: NAEYC.

Yelland, N.J. (2000). *Promoting meaningful learning: Innovations in educating early childhood professionals*. Washington, DC: NAEYC.

Routine Times in the Classroom

Arrival   e.g., Greet each child as he or she arrives each day.

Feeding   e.g., Label foods as they are tasted, "Here is some banana, now let's have a bite of cereal." "You are eating your carrots. Now you are eating a bite of ham."

Nap   e.g., Gaze into the baby's eyes as he or she is rocked to sleep. Sing a lullaby to toddlers as you pat their backs to help them go to sleep

Diaper changing/ Toileting   e.g., Repeat a favorite fingerplay as you diaper the baby or assist toddlers with toileting.

Departure   e.g., Sing a goodbye song as each child leaves.

Strategies for Supporting Emerging Literacy

What teachers do in their classrooms is very important in supporting emerging literacy. Try some of the following strategies in your classroom.

▶ Label your classroom with pictures and words. Both are important. Toddlers can usually read pictures easily, and connecting the picture to the word emphasizes the pattern of the word as well as its letter components. But don't go overboard. Label the important things, starting with 6 to 8 word/picture labels and building up to 12 to 15 over time.

▶ Label storage containers with pictures of what goes inside them. Also label cubbies and coat hooks with pictures and names. And don't forget to label routinely used items such as the bathroom door.

▶ Develop patterning skills by coding shelves with where to put things, particularly the wooden blocks in your classroom. Following a pattern to return blocks to the shelves is an excellent literacy experience as well as an appropriate mathematical experience.

▶ Make and use signs in your classroom. When you leave your classroom to go to the playground, hang a simple sign on the door indicating where you are. When you close an area of the classroom, put a "Closed" sign on it to cue children that the time to play in that area is over. When a child finds something special on the playground or on a nature walk, post a sign that tells everyone about the discovery.

▶ Fill your classroom with "real life" reading materials, such as cookbooks, newspapers, magazines, instruction manuals for toys and materials, appropriate junk mail advertisements, and so on. These are functional reading materials. The children will enjoy the novelty of them and perfect their page-turning skills in the process. And, they will see that reading materials are functional—useful for getting needed information.

▶ Read to the children—individual children, children in small groups of three or four, and occasionally, the whole group. Frequent book reading should be a mainstay of the classroom.

▶ Add books and writing materials to every area of the classroom. When you consider adding or changing an area of the classroom, also think about what kinds of reading and writing materials will go along with the change.

▶ Use narration to connect initial sounds to their word labels.

Strategies for Supporting Emerging Literacy (continued)

▶ Write down children's ideas, words, and stories. When ideas, words, and stories are written down, they take on a special meaning for children (Cooper, 1993; Paley, 1991). Toddlers can learn to dictate the words they want you to add to their work. Offer to do so often. Make your offer open-ended. For example, "Would you like to put some words on your work?" or "What would you like on your work?"

▶ Connect functional writing to children's behavior. For example, when a child does (or doesn't) like something at snack or lunch, tell him that you will let his parents know his preference and go write it on the Communication Sheet. Later, you might ask the child if he would like to write a note to Mom or Dad to let them know about a preference or an idea he had at school. If he agrees, provide a piece of clean paper and a marker or crayon for him to do so. Then, make sure you tell the parent about the importance of the written note by including additional information on the Communication Sheet. Or, if a toddler wants the toy that another child is using, help her write a note to the child to remind her who to give the toy to when she is finished. Put the note near the child and tell her what it says. If the child forgets, point to the note and read it to her.

▶ Explore initial sounds—the beginning sounds of names, words, and toys, objects, and materials. Notice the word exploration. Drills and direct instruction about initial sounds are still inappropriate, but songs, chants, poems, fingerplays, and action rhymes are excellent ways to explore initial sounds. For example, when you call a toddler by name, say, "Rodney, it's your turn to paint with the red paint. The words 'red' and 'Rodney' both start with the same sound." Or, "Caitlin has carrots for lunch. 'Caitlin' and 'carrots' start with the sound /k/." Or, "Thomas is reading a **Thomas the Tank** book. The name of the book and the name of the boy are the same!" Or use fingerplays, rhymes, and songs to reinforce the connection between sounds. "I'm Bringing Home a Baby Bumblebee," for example, is a great song for practicing the initial sound /b/.

This exploration is teacher's work—not children's work. Teachers point out the obvious connections between sounds and letters as they use them in daily experiences. Repeated experiences with adults connecting letters and sounds facilitate phonemic awareness in toddlers that will prepare them for individual letter/sound association when they are older.

Cooper, P. (1993). *When stories come to school: Telling, writing, and performing stories in the early childhood classroom*. New York: Teachers and Writers.
Paley, V.G. (1981). *Wally's stories*. Cambridge, MA: Harvard University Press.

Teacher Competencies to Support Connecting with School and Teacher

Teacher Competencies to Support Connecting with School and Teacher

Sometimes	Usually	Always	
☐	☐	☐	Greets each child and parents upon arrival at school.
☐	☐	☐	Has affectionate, appropriate physical contact with infants.
☐	☐	☐	Moves to children to talk rather than calling from a distance.
☐	☐	☐	Understands how to use voice as a teaching tool by speaking slowly and varying intonation and pitch, and exaggerating vocal transitions.
☐	☐	☐	Accepts cultural differences in children without judgment.
☐	☐	☐	Is alert to signs of fatigue, hunger, and frustration.
☐	☐	☐	Monitors children's general comfort; for example, warmth, dryness, dripping noses, wet chins and chests, and so on.
☐	☐	☐	Listens carefully to infant cries; makes decisions quickly and appropriately; does not allow infants to cry without visual, verbal, and physical responses.
☐	☐	☐	Recognizes that adult mood and facial expressions will be seen and felt by infants and will affect children's experiences and development.
☐	☐	☐	Records accurate information about unusual occurrences, accidents, or changes in children's behavior.

Teacher Competencies to Support Making Friends

Teacher Competencies to Support Making Friends

Sometimes	Usually	Always	
☐	☐	☐	Spends as much or more time listening to parents than providing guidance.
☐	☐	☐	Asks questions to clarify parents' points of view or issues of concern before responding with program policies or procedures.
☐	☐	☐	Comments to parents about strengths, accomplishments, and positive attributes of the child through conversation, notes, phone calls, and so on.
☐	☐	☐	Acknowledges and compliments parents on the unique contributions they make to their child's developmental progress.
☐	☐	☐	Welcomes parents in the classroom at any time during the school day.
☐	☐	☐	Shows she or he likes children and teaching with nonverbal and verbal cues.
☐	☐	☐	Bends over, stoops down, sits, and maintains eye contact while interacting with children.
☐	☐	☐	Uses a low, calm, soothing voice.
☐	☐	☐	Avoids interruption of toddlers' activities; times requests wisely.
☐	☐	☐	Allows toddlers some flexibility in following their own routines; does not insist on scheduling compliance that conflicts with individual schedules.
☐	☐	☐	Makes mealtime and other routine interactions a time for self-help skill practice and social interaction; makes mealtime a pleasant experience.
☐	☐	☐	Actively seeks meaningful exchanges with children.
☐	☐	☐	Uses floor time to build relationships with children.
☐	☐	☐	Plays social games with toddlers.
☐	☐	☐	Takes advantage of opportunities for social play during routines.
☐	☐	☐	Structures periods of social time with other toddlers; remains available to support, facilitate, or interact while toddlers direct the activity.

Techniques for Stimulating Language Development

The field of speech and language development offers several indirect language-stimulation techniques, called description, parallel talk, self-talk, expansion, and expansion plus.

▶ *Description*—Description is a technique in which the teacher narrates or describes what is going on in the child's world by putting word labels on things. For example, if a child looks toward the door as a parent enters the room, the adult might say, "That's Jenny's mother. She must be here to pick up Jenny." Description is also helpful in communicating what Gerber (1979) termed mutual respect. Mutual respect advocates telling children what will happen to them before it happens and waiting for the child to indicate that he is ready. A teacher might say, "It's time for a diaper change" as a description of what will happen to the child. Then, a respectful teacher waits before continuing, so the child can stop his activity and indicate that he is ready. The teacher then describes each step of the diaper change as it occurs.

▶ *Parallel Talk*—Parallel talk is a short phrase that focuses on the child's action. Parallel talk usually begins with "you." For example, "You're turning over from your back to your front" is parallel talk. Other examples might be, "You've got the baby doll" or "You pulled off your shoe." Focusing on the action helps the child put word labels on behavior.

▶ *Self-Talk*—Self-talk focuses on adult behavior—the adult labels and describes what she or he is doing. Teachers who use self-talk usually start their phrases with "I." For example, a teacher might say to a child who is getting fussy, "I'm picking up the toys and then I'll pick you up!"

▶ *Expansion* and *Expansion Plus*—Expansion and expansion plus are extremely useful techniques to use with children when their vocabularies begin to grow. These techniques expand on what the child says (expansion) or add to what the child says (expansion plus). For example, if a child says, "muk," the teacher might say, "You want more milk," or "Jason needs milk, please." This expands on what the child said. Another example of expansion is if a child says, "Outside," the teacher might say, "You'd like to go outside." With expansion plus, the teacher adds a little more to the child's sentence. For example, if a child says, "Go bye-bye," the teacher may say, "It's time to get your things and go bye-bye." Expansion and expansion plus restate what the child says in complete and sometimes expanded sentence form.

Gerber, M. (1979). *Resources for infant educarers: A manual for parents and professionals*. Los Angeles: Resources for Infant Educarers.

Toddler Developmental Tasks

(18 months to 36 months)

Transitioning to School

Making Friends

Exploring Roles

Communicating with Parents, Teachers, and Friends

Problem-solving

Expressing Feelings with Parents, Teachers, and Friends

Using Teacher Competencies to Assess Progress

The teacher competencies in **Innovations** can be used in a number of ways. Mentors or trainers might want to use them to identify a teacher's baseline level of skills, to assess overall levels of competence, or to identify areas for improvement and additional training.

To use the teacher competencies as a baseline measure, ask teachers to conduct self-evaluations of their competencies using the Teachers Competencies from each developmental task. (See pages 46, 108, 176, 243, 318, and 382 in the infant book and pages 56, 140, 226, 307, 390, and 473 in the toddler book or use the combined document on the following pages.) Use the competency lists one at a time for beginning teachers or with teachers with whom you are developing a relationship. Focus on identifying teachers' strengths and areas of competence as well as uncovering areas for further development. More seasoned teachers may want to do a more comprehensive evaluation using all six competency skill lists.

After some experiences with self-evaluation, teachers may be ready for peer evaluation by working cooperatively with a peer to uncover areas for further skill development. Or, the teacher may be ready to form a relationship with a trainer or mentor who can support her or his professional development. If this is the case, always start by observing the teacher at work in her or his classroom. This enables a trainer or mentor to both validate skills and to discover areas for further improvement. The mentor's observations can take the form of anecdotal notes or direct assessment using the competencies.

Finally, in a face-to-face meeting, share your ratings and ask the teacher to share hers or his. Together, identify two or three competencies to begin to work on or develop increased competence. These will form the foundation of a staff development plan that you develop together.

Working Toward Reflective Practice

Developing teaching competence is a lifelong task. Many early childhood educators believe that random training in global training sessions is extremely ineffective. On the other hand, training that is targeted at commonly identified topics within a trusting and mutual relationship results in the most skill growth for teachers.

Although strategies are suggested for both types of training, it is our hope that trainers and mentors will strive to provide much more of the latter type—and in the process, support teachers in becoming reflective practitioners.

Combined List of Infant Teacher Competencies

Teacher Competencies to Support Separating from Parents

☐ ☐ ☐ Looks up, acknowledges, and greets children and parents as they arrive in the classroom.

☐ ☐ ☐ Facilitates child's entry into the classroom and separation from parents as they leave.

☐ ☐ ☐ Accepts and respects each child as she is. Indicates this respect by talking about what is going to happen and waiting for indications of wants or needs before responding.

☐ ☐ ☐ Shows an awareness of each child's temperament and level of development.

☐ ☐ ☐ Responds quickly to children who need attention.

☐ ☐ ☐ Allows children to follow their own schedules; changes with the children as schedules fluctuate. Is an alert observer of each child in the classroom.

☐ ☐ ☐ Uses routines of eating, resting, and diapering as opportunities to maximize reciprocal interactions.

☐ ☐ ☐ Monitors children's general comfort and health (for example, warmth, dryness, noses wiped, wet clothes changed, and so on).

☐ ☐ ☐ Invests in quality time with infants throughout the day during routines and stimulation activities.

☐ ☐ ☐ Uses floor time to build relationships with children.

☐ ☐ ☐ Maintains a positive, pleasant attitude toward parents; thinks in terms of creating a partnership to support the child.

☐ ☐ ☐ Communicates regularly with parents about the child's experience at school; uses a variety of techniques to keep communication flowing freely.

☐ ☐ ☐ Plans, implements, and evaluates regular parent-participation experiences, parent/teacher conferences, and parent-education experiences.

☐ ☐ ☐ Supports children's developing awareness by talking about families, displaying families' photographs, and celebrating accomplishments.

☐ ☐ ☐ Uses books, pictures, and stories to help children identify with events that occur in the world of the family and the school.

Teacher Competencies to Support Connecting with School and Teacher

☐ ☐ ☐ Greets each child and parents upon arrival at school.

☐ ☐ ☐ Has affectionate, appropriate physical contact with infants.

☐ ☐ ☐ Moves to children to talk rather than calling from a distance.

☐ ☐ ☐ Understands how to use voice as a teaching tool by speaking slowly and varying intonation and pitch, and exaggerating vocal transitions.

☐ ☐ ☐ Accepts cultural differences in children without judgment.

☐ ☐ ☐ Is alert to signs of fatigue, hunger, and frustration.

☐ ☐ ☐ Monitors children's general comfort; for example, warmth, dryness, dripping noses, wet chins and chests, and so on.

☐ ☐ ☐ Listens carefully to infant cries; makes decisions quickly and appropriately; does not allow infants to cry without visual, verbal, and physical responses.

☐ ☐ ☐ Recognizes that adult mood and facial expressions will be seen and felt by infants and will affect children's experiences and development.

☐ ☐ ☐ Records accurate information about unusual occurrences, accidents, or changes in children's behavior.

Teacher Competencies to Support Relating to Self and Others

☐ ☐ ☐ Spends as much or more time listening to parents than providing guidance.

☐ ☐ ☐ Asks questions to clarify parents' points of view or issues of concern before responding with program policies or procedures.

☐ ☐ ☐ Comments to parents about strengths, accomplishments, and positive attributes of the child through conversation, notes, phone calls, and so on.

☐ ☐ ☐ Acknowledges and compliments parents on the unique contributions they make to their child's developmental progress.

☐ ☐ ☐ Welcomes parents in the classroom at any time during the school day.

☐ ☐ ☐ Shows she or he likes children and teaches with nonverbal and verbal cues.

☐ ☐ ☐ Bends over, stoops down, sits, maintains eye contact while interacting with infants.

☐ ☐ ☐ Uses a low, calm, soothing voice.

☐ ☐ ☐ Avoids interruption of infants' activities; times requests wisely.

☐ ☐ ☐ Allows infants to follow their own routines; does not insist on scheduling compliance that conflicts with individual schedules.

☐ ☐ ☐ Makes mealtime and other routine interactions a time for sensory stimulation, self-help skill practice, and social interaction.

☐ ☐ ☐ Actively seeks meaningful exchanges with children.

☐ ☐ ☐ Uses floor time to build relationships with children.

☐ ☐ ☐ Responds to social gestures and noises of infants and elaborates on the interactions.

☐ ☐ ☐ Plays responsive social games.

☐ ☐ ☐ Takes advantage of opportunities for social play during routines.

☐ ☐ ☐ Structures periods of social time with other infants; remains available to support, facilitate, or interact while infants direct the activity.

Teacher Competencies to Support Communicating with Parents, Teachers, and Friends

☐ ☐ ☐ States directions in positive terms.

☐ ☐ ☐ Communicates effectively with children and adults.

☐ ☐ ☐ Speaks in simple, understandable terms.

☐ ☐ ☐ Understands how to use voice as a teaching tool.

☐ ☐ ☐ Mediates communication between children to foster social communication and interaction.

☐ ☐ ☐ Uses nonverbal techniques to communicate desired behavior.

☐ ☐ ☐ Uses existing materials and equipment effectively.

☐ ☐ ☐ Devises new materials to stimulate and challenge children.

☐ ☐ ☐ Rotates and adapts materials to insure children's interest.

☐ ☐ ☐ Encourages language by repeating infant vocalizations, adding new sounds, naming objects, expanding the child's language, and narrating events relevant to the child.

☐ ☐ ☐ Avoids baby talk. Uses "parentese," the high-pitched, slow-paced, exaggerated enunciations that make speech easier for babies to understand.

☐ ☐ ☐ Uses language in context without unnecessary repetitions.

☐ ☐ ☐ Responds to infant communications in a variety of ways such as vocalizations, facial expressions, and body language.

Teacher Competencies to Support Learning to Move

☐ ☐ ☐ Is aware of the activities of the entire group even when dealing with a part of it; positions self strategically, looks up often from involvement.

☐ ☐ ☐ Establishes and carries out reasonable limits for children and activities.

☐ ☐ ☐ Uses nonpunitive ways of dealing with behavior; can exert authority without requiring submission or undermining the child's sense of self.

☐ ☐ ☐ Redirects, distracts, or channels inappropriate behavior into acceptable outlets. Anticipates confrontations between children and intervenes before aggressive behavior arises.

☐ ☐ ☐ Anticipates problems and plans to prevent their re-occurence.

☐ ☐ ☐ Does not avoid problem situations, can generate alternative ideas, and implement and evaluate solutions selected.

☐ ☐ ☐ Reinforces appropriate behavior by encouraging children's appropriate behavior.

☐ ☐ ☐ Uses praise and encouragement effectively; differentiates between the behavior and the child when using praise.

☐ ☐ ☐ Guides children to work out increasingly effective ways of making social contacts and solving social problems.

☐ ☐ ☐ Sees that children are dressed appropriately for existing temperatures throughout the day.

☐ ☐ ☐ Models the behavior being encouraged and taught to children.

☐ ☐ ☐ Assures that all children have frequent opportunities for success.

☐ ☐ ☐ Provides regular and varied outdoor experience.

☐ ☐ ☐ Provides ample opportunity for and encouragement of large muscle activity.

☐ ☐ ☐ Knows a variety of guidance techniques such as redirection, distraction, ignoring, using room arrangements and schedules to support appropriate behavior, and uses each appropriately.

☐ ☐ ☐ Helps parents develop realistic expectations for children's behavior in ways that help avoid disciplinary problems.

Teacher Competencies to Support Expressing Feelings with Parents, Teachers, and Friends

☐ ☐ ☐ Checks infants periodically for wetness; asks the child first if he needs changing.

☐ ☐ ☐ Assures that children have frequent opportunities for success. Delights in each child's success, expresses kindness and support when children are struggling with developmental challenges, and supports children in learning from their mistakes.

☐ ☐ ☐ Uses vocabulary, materials, activities, and experiences that are suitable for the age, stage, temperament, and learning styles of children in her or his group.

☐ ☐ ☐ Exhibits flexibility in carrying out activity and experience plans.

☐ ☐ ☐ Shows imagination and spontaneity in building on children's interests for developing curriculum rather than depending exclusively on pre-prepared curriculum.

☐ ☐ ☐ Plans, implements, and evaluates parent-teacher conferences, intake interviews, and gradual enrollment.

☐ ☐ ☐ Plans, implements, and evaluates parent-participation activities.

☐ ☐ ☐ Models the recognition and expression of feelings by naming her or his own feelings.

☐ ☐ ☐ Uses modeling and patterning as strategies for helping babies interact successfully.

☐ ☐ ☐ Understands that social roles and expectations for children in their family setting may be different from what is expected at school. Helps children make the transition between these two different sets of expectations and helps children behave appropriately in each.

☐ ☐ ☐ Serves as a social model by building a relationship with each child and family and by maintaining positive relationships with other teachers. Provides children with a break from social interaction or over-stimulation as needed.

☐ ☐ ☐ Watches and observes children at play and throughout the school day.

Combined List of Toddler Teacher Competencies

INNOVATIONS

Teacher Competencies to Support Transitioning to School

☐ ☐ ☐ Looks up, acknowledges, and greets children and parents as they arrive in the class room.

☐ ☐ ☐ Facilitates child's entry into the classroom and separation from parents as they leave.

☐ ☐ ☐ Accepts and respects each child as she is. Indicates this respect by talking about what is going to happen and waiting for indications of wants or needs before responding.

☐ ☐ ☐ Shows an awareness of each child's temperament and level of development.

☐ ☐ ☐ Responds quickly to children who need attention.

☐ ☐ ☐ Allows children to follow their own schedules; changes with the children as schedules fluctuate. Is an alert observer of each child in the classroom.

☐ ☐ ☐ Uses routines of eating, resting, and diapering as opportunities to maximize reciprocal interactions.

☐ ☐ ☐ Monitors children's general comfort and health (for example, warmth, dryness, noses wiped, wet clothes changed, and so on).

☐ ☐ ☐ Invests in quality time with infants throughout the day during routines and stimulation activities.

☐ ☐ ☐ Uses floor time to build relationships with children.

☐ ☐ ☐ Maintains a positive, pleasant attitude toward parents; thinks in terms of creating a partnership to support the child.

☐ ☐ ☐ Communicates regularly with parents about the child's experience at school; uses a variety of techniques to keep communication flowing freely.

☐ ☐ ☐ Plans, implements, and evaluates regular parent participation experiences, parent/teacher conferences, and parent education experiences.

☐ ☐ ☐ Supports children's developing awareness by talking about families, displaying families' photographs, and celebrating accomplishments.

☐ ☐ ☐ Uses books, pictures, and stories to help children identify with events that occur in the world of the family and the school.

Teacher Competencies to Support Making Friends

☐ ☐ ☐ Spends as much or more time listening to parents than providing guidance.

☐ ☐ ☐ Asks questions to clarify parents' points of view or issues of concern before responding with program policies or procedures.

☐ ☐ ☐ Comments to parents about strengths, accomplishments, and positive attributes of the child through conversation, notes, phone calls, and so on.

☐ ☐ ☐ Acknowledges and compliments parents on the unique contributions they make to their child's developmental progress.

☐ ☐ ☐ Welcomes parents in the classroom at any time during the school day.

☐ ☐ ☐ Shows she or he likes children and teaching with nonverbal and verbal cues.

☐ ☐ ☐ Bends over, stoops down, sits, and maintains eye contact while interacting with children.

☐ ☐ ☐ Uses a low, calm, soothing voice.

☐ ☐ ☐ Avoids interruption of toddlers' activities; times requests wisely.

☐ ☐ ☐ Allows toddlers some flexibility in following their own routines; does not insist on scheduling compliance that conflicts with individual schedules.

☐ ☐ ☐ Makes mealtime and other routine interactions a time for self-help skill practice and social interaction; makes mealtime a pleasant experience.

☐ ☐ ☐ Actively seeks meaningful exchanges with children.

☐ ☐ ☐ Uses floor time to build relationships with children.

☐ ☐ ☐ Plays social games with toddlers.

☐ ☐ ☐ Takes advantage of opportunities for social play during routines.

☐ ☐ ☐ Structures periods of social time with other toddlers; remains available to support, facilitate, or interact while toddlers direct the activity.

Teacher Competencies to Support Exploring Roles

☐ ☐ ☐ Shows support for parents as primary educators by developing partnership of respect, information exchange, and collaboration.

☐ ☐ ☐ Finds many different ways for family members to be involved in the school experience of the child.

☐ ☐ ☐ Recognizes, accepts, and celebrates cultural differences.

☐ ☐ ☐ Recognizes and acknowledges the unique contributions that parents make to their child's developmental progress.

☐ ☐ ☐ ***Does not treat every child the same***—bases interactions and teaching on understanding of each child's developmental age and stage as well as on the child's uniqueness.

☐ ☐ ☐ Supports children's feelings of belonging—all children belong in the classroom.

☐ ☐ ☐ Uses encouragement (instead of praise) to describe completed tasks.

☐ ☐ ☐ Validates children's uniqueness, focusing on positive feelings about their unique qualities.

☐ ☐ ☐ Provides opportunities for exploration, investigation, and development of new alternatives.

☐ ☐ ☐ Assures that interactions in the classroom are characterized by mutual respect.

☐ ☐ ☐ Helps children handle failure by being close and recognizing effort.

☐ ☐ ☐ Is an ally to help identify potential solutions to solving problems.

Teacher Competencies to Support Communicating with Parents, Teachers, and Friends

☐ ☐ ☐ States directions in positive terms.

☐ ☐ ☐ Communicates effectively with children and adults.

☐ ☐ ☐ Speaks in simple, understandable terms.

☐ ☐ ☐ Understands how to use voice as a teaching tool.

☐ ☐ ☐ Uses nonverbal techniques to communicate desired behavior.

☐ ☐ ☐ Uses existing materials and equipment effectively.

☐ ☐ ☐ Devises new materials to stimulate and challenge children.

☐ ☐ ☐ Rotates and adapts materials to insure children's interest.

☐ ☐ ☐ Encourages language by expanding sentences used by toddlers.

☐ ☐ ☐ Narrates routines throughout the day.

☐ ☐ ☐ Makes and keeps eye contact with toddlers.

☐ ☐ ☐ Talks with toddlers, labeling objects, pointing out actions, and

☐ ☐ ☐ describing actions and reactions.

☐ ☐ ☐ Waits for responses to questions.

☐ ☐ ☐ Asks simple, open-ended questions that require a real response.

Teacher Competencies to Support Learning to Solve Problems

☐ ☐ ☐ Is aware of the activities of the entire group even when dealing with a part of it; positions self strategically, looks up often from involvement.

☐ ☐ ☐ Establishes and carries out reasonable limits for children and activities.

☐ ☐ ☐ Uses nonpunitive ways of dealing with behavior; can exert authority without requiring submission or undermining the child's sense of self.

☐ ☐ ☐ Redirects, distracts, or channels inappropriate behavior into acceptable outlets.

☐ ☐ ☐ Anticipates confrontations between children and intervenes before aggressive behavior arises.

☐ ☐ ☐ Anticipates problems and plans to prevent their reccurrence.

☐ ☐ ☐ Does not avoid problem situations; can generate alternative ideas, and implement and evaluate solutions selected.

☐ ☐ ☐ Reinforces appropriate behavior by encouraging children's appropriate behavior.

☐ ☐ ☐ Uses praise and encouragement effectively; differentiates between the behavior and the child when using praise.

☐ ☐ ☐ Guides children to work out increasingly effective ways of making social contacts and solving social problems.

☐ ☐ ☐ Sees that children are dressed appropriately for existing temperatures throughout the day.

☐ ☐ ☐ Models the behavior being encouraged and taught to children.

☐ ☐ ☐ Assures that all children have frequent opportunities for success.

☐ ☐ ☐ Provides regular and varied outdoor experience.

Teacher Competencies to Support Expressing Feelings with Parents, Teachers, and Friends

☐ ☐ ☐ Checks toddlers periodically for wetness, asks the child first if he needs changing; reminds toddlers to check their bodies to see if they need to toilet, helps toddlers with toilet play as well as toilet training.

☐ ☐ ☐ Assures that children have frequent opportunities for success. Delights in each child's success, expresses kindness and support when children are struggling with developmental challenges, and supports children in learning from their mistakes.

☐ ☐ ☐ Invites children to play with each other; participates in play as a partner and a facilitator.

☐ ☐ ☐ Allows children to direct and manage their own play.

☐ ☐ ☐ Recognizes the toddlers' need for balance between independence and dependence.

☐ ☐ ☐ Uses vocabulary, materials, activities, and experiences that are suitable for the age, stage, temperament, and learning styles of children in her or his group.

☐ ☐ ☐ Exhibits flexibility in carrying out activity and experience plans.

☐ ☐ ☐ Shows imagination and spontaneity in building on children's interest for developing curriculum rather than depending exclusively on pre-prepared curriculum.

☐ ☐ ☐ Plans, implements, and evaluates parent-teacher conferences, intake interviews, and gradual enrollment.

☐ ☐ ☐ Models the recognition and expression of feelings by naming her or his own feelings.

Value of Play Chart

Possibility	Fine and Gross Motor Development	Quantitative Thinking	Conceptualizing	Aesthetic Appreciation	Language/ Literacy Development
Dramatic	Household tasks, stacking bowls/dishes, dressing/undressing dolls, pushing buggy, dressing/undressing themselves, filling and dumping purses, bags	Grouping, sorting, measuring, one-to-one correspondence, counting	Writing notes/numerals, labeling, playing with play money	Pictures, clothes, decorations	Dramatic play, role playing, discussion, questioning
Sensory/Art	Drawing, manipulating, touching, pouring, moving, sifting, scooping pulling, grasping	Grouping, sorting, measuring, one-to-one correspondence, counting	Objects as symbols, labels, creating stories	Designs, movement, creative expression, decorations	Discussion, questioning, problem-solving, describing, naming, explaining
Curiosity	Picking up, pulling, moving, shaking, rolling, opening, manipulating	Grouping, comparing, one-to-one correspondence, matching, counting	Recognition, writing, geometric forms	Design, shape, size, color, light/dark, form	Discussion, questioning, problem-solving, naming
Construction (for toddlers)	Pulling, grasping, pushing, stacking, opening	Counting, grouping, sorting, one-to-one correspondence	Signs on buildings, blocks as symbols, labels, creating a story	Design, size, color, shape, form	Discussion, labeling, problem-solving, naming, questioning
Literacy	Hand and finger control	Comparing, grouping, sound/letter recognition	Labels, names, signs	Interpretation, empathy, expression	Vocabulary, sound/letter recognition, conversation, dramatic play
Music/Movement	Clapping, bouncing, singing, movements to songs/fingerplays	Counting, comparing, measuring	Words to songs and fingerplays, movements	Creative dance and movements	Singing songs, saying fingerplays
Outdoor	Pushing, carrying, dancing, climbing, pedaling, running, jumping	Counting, comparing, measuring, matching, sorting, one-to-one correspondence	Labels, names, signs	Creative dance and movements, role playing, expression	Conversation, questioning, problem-solving
Projects	Practicing and perfecting techniques	Counting, comparing, measuring, matching, sorting, one-to-one correspondence	Representing ideas, labels, signs, creating	Expression, design, shape, size, color, form	Conversation, questioning, problem-solving

Workshop Evaluation
for Participants (version 1)

Using a rating scale of 1 (poor) to 5 (excellent), evaluate the following areas:

Usefulness of content	1	2	3	4	5
Knowledge and style of presenter	1	2	3	4	5
Environment for workshop	1	2	3	4	5
Usefulness of materials	1	2	3	4	5

I will apply what I learned today by

I need more information on

Comments/ideas for improvement

Workshop Evaluation
for Participants (version 2)

Today I learned

My favorite part of the workshop was

My least favorite part of the workshop was

Overall, I would rate the workshop

1 (a waste of time) to 5 (extremely helpful)

1   2   3   4   5

Comments

Workshop Evaluation
for Presenters

Today I learned

Setting

How did the setting support/detract from the presentation?

Workshop Presentation

Did I start on time?

Did I give an overview of the content for the teachers?

Did I allow the teachers to help mold the content/direction of the workshop?

Which techniques worked best?

Which techniques need to be rethought?

Was the presentation organized and logical?

Was I able to establish rapport with the participants?

Did I allow enough time to cover all the major points adequately?

Was I enthusiastic about the topic?

Did I show the teachers the importance/usefulness of information in the workshop?

Did I summarize the major points?

Did I end on time?

Did the teachers know how to apply what they learned?

How would I change this workshop for next time?

The best part of the workshop was

The worst part of the workshop was

Overall, I would rate the workshop
1 (a waste of time) to 5 (extremely helpful)
1   2   3   4   5

Comments

INNOVATIONS

TRAINING CERTIFICATE

Certificate of Training Completion

is awarded to

NAME

WORKSHOP TITLE

HOURS CREDIT

INSTRUCTOR

LOCATION

DATE

INNOVATIONS

Innovations

Combined Infant and Toddler
Observation/Assessment
Birth-3 years

CHILD'S NAME   TEACHER

Infant (0-18 months) Assessment

Task: Separating from Parents

	0-6 months	6-12 months		12-18 months
S1	a. Little or no experience with separating from Mom and Dad; accepts sensitive care from substitute.	b. Some experience with separating from Mom and Dad; prefers familiar caregiver, but accepts sensitive care from substitute.	c. More experience with separating from Mom and Dad; resists separating; shows distress upon separation, and takes time to adjust.	d. Experienced with separating from Mom and Dad; resists initial separation, but adjusts after only a few moments.
S2	a. Startled by new sounds, smells, and people.	b. Orients toward new or interesting stimuli.		c. Seeks new and interesting stimuli.
S3	a. Accepts transitions without notice.	b. Reacts with discomfort during the transition.	c. Resists transition preparation as well as the transition.	d. Anticipates transitions when preparation activities begin. If preparation is to a preferred, familiar activity, transition is accepted.
S4	a. Displays indiscriminate attachment; will accept sensitive care from most familiar adults; exhibits preference for Mom, Dad, or familiar caregiver if present.	b. Displays discriminate attachment; will still accept care from sensitive caregivers, but prefers care from Mom, Dad, or familiar caregivers.		c. Separation anxiety emerges; resists approaches by unfamiliar adults and resists separation from Mom, Dad, and familiar caregivers. Cries, clings, calls for parents when they leave the child's view.
S5	a. Unpredictable daily schedule.	b. Patterns in daily schedule emerge around eating and sleeping.		c. Daily schedule is predictable. Eating and sleeping patterns are relatively stable and predictable.
S6	a. Feeds from breast or bottle.	b. Begins to take baby food from a spoon; begins to sip from a cup.		c. Drinks from bottle and/or cup; eats finger foods.
S7	a. Plays with objects within visual field; bats at objects with hands and feet.	b. Manipulates, mouths, and plays with objects; likes action/reaction toys. Plays with objects then drops them to move on to new objects. May return to objects again and again.		c. Plays with favorite things again and again. Likes to dump out objects and play with them on the floor. Considers all objects and toys in the environment personal play choices, even when being played with by others.

Toddler (18-36 months) Assessment

Task: Transitioning to School

	18-24 months	24-30 months		30-36 months
T1	a. Experienced in separating from Mom and Dad; may resist initial separation in new or unusual settings, but adjusts after a few moments.	b. Experienced with separating; looks forward to favorite activities. May approach new or unusual settings with caution, but gets interested after a few minutes.		c. Separates easily in most situations. If cautious, gets over caution quickly when invited to join in by a friendly adult or peer.
T2	a. Actively seeks new and interesting stimuli; interested in everything in the environment.	b. May get into difficulty seeking and exploring interesting stimuli (e.g., climbing on furniture, opening off-limits cabinets).		c. Seeks novel and interesting stimuli; when presented with familiar and novel stimuli, prefers novel ones.
T3	a. Resists separations and transitions to unfamiliar or new settings or to settings that are not preferred.	b. Transitions to familiar people in familiar settings easily; still cautious about unfamiliar settings or new experiences.		c. Transitions to most settings without distress; when distress occurs, can be comforted or redirected.
T4	a. Separation anxiety begins to resolve; is able to make transitions to familiar settings with familiar adults without experiencing distress. When distress occurs, it resolves when the child gets interested in the new setting and playmates.	b. Stranger anxiety emerges. Fear of strangers and new situations causes proximity-seeking behavior such as getting close to primary caregiver, clinging, crying, resistance of social overtures (e.g., hiding behind adult, hiding face).		c. Stranger anxiety begins resolving; may continue to be cautious, but will accept interactions from strangers after watching or observing for a moment. Takes cues (looks to them, watches their reactions) about new situations from familiar adults.
T5	a. Prefers predictable routines and schedule; manages changes in schedule fairly well at the time but may experience problems later.	b. Ritualistic about routines and schedule—likes routines predictably "just so"; exhibits ritualistic behavior around routines; likes routines the same way every time; needs warnings of anticipated transitions and still may resist them; melts down or tantrums when schedule is changed without reminders and preparation.		c. Adapts to changes in schedule when prepared in advance; abrupt or unplanned schedule changes still present problems; adapts more readily in familiar settings except when tired, hungry, or ill.
T6	a. Tries new food when presented; has strong food preferences.	b. Resists new foods on some days and not on others; reduces intake; may become a picky eater or refuse to try new foods when offered.	c. Has small selection of food preferences; still resists new food when presented; eats well on some days and not on others.	d. Food intake and preferences even out; will try new food after many presentations; needs encouragement to try new foods.
T7	a. Develops a sense of property rights; hoards toys and favorite objects.	b. Considers objects being played with as personal property.		c. Recognizes mine and not mine.

Infant (0-18 months) Assessment

Task: Connecting with School and Teacher

	0-6 months		6-12 months	12-18 months
C1	a. Does not resist separating from parents.		b. Resists separating from parents; resists comfort from primary teacher.	c. Resists separating from parents; accepts comfort from primary teacher.
C2	a. Accepts transition from parent to teacher.		b. Maintains physical proximity to primary teacher during separation.	c. Seeks primary teacher's support in separating.
C3	a. Comforts after a period of distress.		b. Comforts quickly after being picked up.	c. Comforts when needs or wants are acknowledged by caregiver.
C4	a. Is unaware of friends in classroom.		b. Visually notices friends in classroom.	c. Gets excited about seeing friends; seeks physical proximity.
C5	a. Uses parents and teacher physically to support exploration of the environment; explores objects placed nearby parents and teachers.		b. Uses parents and teacher visually to support exploration of the environment; manipulates objects found in environment.	c. Explores the environment independently; responds to play cues presented by adults.
C6	a. Focuses on face-to-face interaction.	b. Tracks moving object up and down and right to left.	c. Watches people, objects, and activities in immediate environment.	d. Initiates interactions with people, toys, and the environment.
C7	a. Objects exist only when in view.	b. Objects perceived as having separate existence.	c. Looks where objects were last seen after they disappear.	d. Follows visual displacement of objects.
C8	a. Thinks object disappears when it moves out of view.	b. Looks where object was last seen after it disappears.	c. Follows object as it disappears.	d. Searches for hidden object if the disappearance was observed.

Toddler (18-36 months) Assessment

Task: Making Friends

	18-24 months	24-30 months	30-36 months
MF1	a. Calms self with verbal support from adults and transitional objects.	b. Calms self with verbal support from adults; may look for transitional objects to help with the calm-down process after verbal support is provided. Frequency of emotional outburst begins to diminish.	c. Calms self with only verbal support. Use of transitional objects begins to decline except at bedtime and when recovering from intense emotional outbursts.
MF2	a Goes to mirror to look at self; makes faces, and shows emotions like laughing, crying, and so on.	b. Calls own name when looking at photographs or in the mirror.	c. Calls names of friends in photographs.
MF3	a. Develops preferences for types of play and types of toys.	b. Develops play themes that are repeated again and again (such as mommy or firefighter).	c. Begins exploration of a wider range of play themes. Themes often come from new experiences.
MF4	a. Perfects gross motor skills such as running, climbing, and riding push toys. Fine motor skills with manipulatives (simple puzzles, Duplos, and so on) are emerging.	b. Likes physical challenges such as running fast, jumping high, and going up and down stairs. Plays with preferred manipulatives for increasing periods of time.	c. Competently exhibits a wide range of physical skills. Begins to be interested in practicing skills such as throwing a ball, riding a tricycle, or completing a puzzle.
MF5	a. Play may be onlooker, solitary, or parallel in nature.	b. Play is predominantly parallel in nature.	c. Exhibits associative play with familiar play partners.
MF6	a. Exhibits symbolic play.	b. Practices and explores a wide variety of symbolic play themes and roles.	
MF7	a. Objects to strangers presence; clings, cries, and seeks support when strangers are around.	b. Objection to strangers begins to diminish; may still be wary of strangers or new situations.	c. Is able to venture into strange or new situations if prepared in advance and supported by adults.
MF8	a. Uses single words to indicate needs and wants such as "muk" for "I want milk," or "bye bye" for "Let's go bye bye."	b. Uses phrases and 2- to 3-word sentences to indicate needs and wants.	c. Uses 4- to 6-word sentences to indicate needs and wants.
MF9	a. Connects emotions with behaviors; uses language to express these connections.	b. Uses emotional ideas in play. c. Elaborates on emotional ideas and understanding to play with objects.	d. Begins emotional thinking; begins to understand emotional cause-and-effect relationships.
MF10	a. Takes turns with toys and materials with adult support and facilitation.	b. Takes turns with toys and materials with friend, sometimes without adult support.	
MF11	a. Experiments with behavior that accomplishes a goal; may bite, pinch, poke, scratch, push, and so on while trying to make things happen.	b. Begins to anticipate what might happen when actions are taken; chooses to make things happen if outcomes are desirable (e.g., trade toys with a friend who will stay and play), and resists taking action if outcomes are undesirable (e.g., teacher putting markers away if child chews on the tips).	

Infant (0-18 months) Assessment

Task: Relating to Self and Others

	0-6 months	6-12 months		12-18 months
R1	a. Calms self with adult support	b. Calms self with support from adults and/or transitional objects.		c. Calms self with transitional objects.
R2	a. Unaware of own image in mirror.	b. Curious about own image in mirrors and photographs.	c. Discovers self in mirror and photographs.	d. Differentiates own image from images of others.
R3	a. Begins to demonstrate preferences for different types of sensory stimuli.	b. Prefers some types of stimuli to others.		c. Is interested in pursuing favorite stimulation activities again and again.
R4	a. Develops a multi-sensory interest in the world—wants to see, touch, mouth, hear, and hold objects.	b. Uses senses to explore and discover the near environment.		c. Uses motor movements to enhance sensory exploration of the environment.
R5	a. Play is predominantly unoccupied in nature.	b. Play is predominantly onlooker in nature.	c. Play is predominantly solitary in nature.	
R6	a. Exhibits practice play.			b. Exhibits symbolic play.
R7	a. Develops an interest in the human world.	b. Seeks interactions with responsive adults; interested also in what other children are doing.	c. Seeks most interactions with familiar adults; fascinated by what other children are doing.	d. Prefers interactions with familiar adults; resists interaction with unfamiliar adults; may be cautious with unfamiliar friends.
R8	a. Does not distinguish between needs (social interaction, a new position, holding instead of lying in the bed) and wants (food, diaper changes, sleep).	b. Begins to distinguish between needs and wants; can communicate differently about different needs and wants.	c. Uses objects, gestures, and behaviors to indicate needs and wants.	d. Uses single words to indicate needs and wants like "muk" for "I want milk", or bye-bye for "Let's go bye-bye."
R9	a. Creates mental images of emotions and emotional responses to situations.			b. Begins to understand how feelings relate to others
R10	a. Unable to negotiate interactions with peers without direct adult support and facilitation.	b. Calls for help loudly by crying or screaming when problems occur during exploration of the environment or with peers.	c. Exchanges or trades with peers to get a desired toy or material with direct adult support and facilitation.	d. Asks other children to walk away when conflict arises between children; expects the other child to do so.
R11	a. Explores environment and the things in it orally. May bite, poke, scratch, or pinch others during exploration.			b. Experiments with behavior that gets a reaction; may bite, pinch, poke, scratch during interactions with others to see what happens.

Toddler (18-36 months) Assessment

Task: Exploring Roles

	18-24 months	24-30 months	30-36 months
ER1	a. Explores roles related to self and family.	b. Explores roles related to self, friends, family, and neighborhood.	c. Explores roles related to self, friends, family, neighborhood, and the community at large.
ER2	a. Is unable to choose or modify behavior in response to physical or social cues of situations; persists in using behavior that doesn't work in situations.	b. Begins to choose or modify behavior in response to physical and social cues of situations; when one behavior isn't working, may stop and try something else.	c. Chooses and modifies behavior in response to the physical and social cues of a situation; tries to choose the behaviors that will get what he or she wants; can change behaviors if they are not working.
ER3	a. Does not understand the impact of own behavior on others.	b. Begins to understand the impact of own behavior on others; shows interest and awareness of the emotional behaviors of friends and others.	c. Understands the impact of own behavior on others; anticipates how friends or others will react.
ER4	a. Uses props to play roles; becomes the occupant of the role (is superman when wearing a cape or mommy when holding a baby). Prefers familiar roles.	b. Uses props to adopt roles; abandons roles when the props are removed; changes between familiar and favorite roles in dramatic play.	c. Can play roles with or without props. Transitions between roles frequently and easily (e.g., can be the mommy, then the daddy, then the monster during same play period).

Infant (0-18 months) Assessment

Task: Communicating with Parents, Teachers, and Friends

	0-6 months			6-12 months		12-18 months	
CM1	a. Gazes at familiar faces.	b. Responds to facial expressions of familiar faces.	c. Occasionally engages in reciprocal communication with facial expressions, vowel sounds, and voice inflection.	d. Frequently engages in reciprocal communication using facial expressions, inflection, and vowel and consonant sounds.		e. Imitates and jabbers in response to familiar voices.	
CM2	a. Makes sounds	b. Imitiates intonational and inflectional vocal patterns.		c. Develops holophrasic speech—words that convey complete sentences or thoughts.	d. Uses the same word to convey different meaning.	e. Develops telegraphic speech where 2 or 3 words are used as a sentence.	
CM3	a. Listens to familiar people's voices when they talk.	b. Shows understanding of simple phrases by responding or reacting.		c. Points or looks at familiar objects when asked to do so.		d. Follows commands with visual cues or context cues.	
CM4	a. Babbles motorically, acoustically, and visually simple sounds like (m), (p), (b), (n) at the beginning of words and vowel sounds like (ah), (oh), (uh).			b. Babbles sounds like (w), (k), (f), (t), (d) at the beginning of words and vowels sounds like (eh), (ee); strings sounds together (ba-ba-ba-ba-ba) and practices sounds in a wide variety of ways.			
CM5	a. Responds discriminantly to voices of mother and father.	b. Turns toward and responds to familiar voices and sounds.		c. Prefers familiar sounds and voices.		d. Directs vocalizations toward familiar people and objects in the environment.	
CM6	a. Experiments with babbling and cooing.	b. Inflection is added to babbling and cooing.				c. Single words or phrases are understandable to familiar adults; strangers may not understand these words.	
CM7	a. Looks at picture books.	b. Listens to books when read by a familiar adult.				c. Points to pictures.	d. Turns pages.

Toddler (18-36 months) Assessment

Task: *Communicating with Parents, Teachers, and Friends*

	18-24 months	24-30 months	30-36 months
CM1	a. Expressive vocabulary increases; uses about 200 words on a regular basis. Expressive language continues to be telegraphic, where single words may carry expanded meaning only understood by familiar caregivers.	b. Vocabulary size begins to grow rapidly; sentence length begins to increase with 3 or 4 words in some sentences.	c. Sentence length continues to grow. Four- to six-word sentences predominate expressive language. Vocabulary continues to expand; expressive vocabulary is adequate to make most needs and wants understood by others.
CM2	a. Uses a greater variety of sounds and sound combinations, simplifying the word if it is too complex (such as pane for plane, tephone for telephone); enjoys experimenting with inflection that sounds like adult speech although it is not yet understandable.	b. Rapid development of new sound combinations and new words that are understandable to adults. Uses language functionally—to ask for things and get needs met and to interact with friends.	c. Is able to use language to get most needs and wants met by familiar caregivers and to interact with friends.
CM3	a. Seeks vocal interactions with familiar people; can communicate needs and wants to familiar caregivers; begins to be wary of talking to strangers.	b. Resists interactions with strangers; hides, withdraws, or objects to encouragement to talk to strangers.	
CM4	a. 20-25% of language is intelligible to strangers. Parents and caregivers can understand more.	b. 60-65% of language is intelligible to strangers. Parents and caregivers understand most of the child's expressive language.	
CM5	a. "Reads" book from front to back; turns books right side up to look at them. b. Makes sounds that connect to pictures in books.	c. Listens to a complete story from beginning to end; asks to read familiar books over and over again.	d. Likes to look at books independently; "reads" books to self.
CM6	a. Actively experiments with the environment; follows visual displacement of objects.	b. Begins transition to symbolic thought. Uses formed mental images to solve problems. Thought processes relate to concrete experiences and objects.	c. Begins transition to pre-operational stage characterized by the beginning of symbolic thought and the use of mental images and words.

Infant (0-18 months) Assessment

Task: Moving Around Home and School

	0-6 months						6-12 months				12-18 months					
M1	a. Holds head away from shoulder.	b. Holds head steady side to side.	c. Holds head up when lying on stomach.	d. Rolls from back to front.	e. Rolls from front to back.	f. Scoots on stomach.	g. Sits with support.	h. Sits without support.	i. Crawls after ball or toy.	j. Pulls to a stand.	k. Lowers back down to squatting position.	l. Walks with support.	m. Walks without support.	n. Squats down and stands back up.	o. Climbs into chair.	p. Kicks ball.
M2	a. Eyes and head follow motion.	b. Holds rattle.	c. Exchanges objects between hands.	d. Uses pincher grasp to pick up small items.	e. Picks up toys and objects.	f. Dumps objects out of containers.	g. Puts objects back into containers.	h. Scribbles.			i. Turns pages in cardboard book.	j. Unbuttons large buttons.	k. Completes puzzles with 2-3 pieces.			

Toddler (18-36 months) Assessment

Task: Problem-solving

	18-24 months	24-30 months	30-36 months
PS1	a. Interest in toileting is limited to watching; may show interest in flushing toilet, sitting on the toilet, or washing hands. Interest may wax and wane quickly.	b. Toilet play stage of toileting; interested in playing at toileting activities such as taking off diaper, sitting on the toilet, using toilet paper, flushing the toilet, and washing hands.	c. Toilet practice begins; likes to repeat toileting activities again and again, with or without success.
PS2	a. Activity level increases; requests and seeks out motor activities. Does not control activity level without adult support; yet resists adult support in modulating activity level.	b. Activity level continues to increase; continues to seek out motor activities. Begins to modulate activity levels with verbal and physical adult support (e.g., slow down, take a deep breath).	c. Alternates between high levels of activity and periods of calm, quieter activity. Can modulate activity level with verbal reminders from adults.
PS3	a. On-task behavior begins to increase.	b. Able to sustain favorite activities for increasingly longer periods of time; extends on-task play time at favorite activities to 10 minutes. Still loses interest in other activities quickly.	c. Stays on task at favorite manipulative activities for sustained periods of time; extends on-task play time at favorite activities to 20 minutes. Still loses interest in other activities quickly.
PS4	a. Carries toys around from place to place. b. Undresses; takes off shoes, socks, and clothes. c. Turns door knob to open door.	d. Holds cup with one hand to drink. e. Shows preference for one hand.	f. Unzips zipper. g. Pulls pants up. h. Zips zipper.
PS5	a. Propels riding toys with feet. b. Runs; collapses to stop forward movement.	c. Goes up stairs without alternating feet, holding on to handrail. d. Runs; begins to control starting and stopping. e. Balances on one foot.	f. Goes up stairs alternating feet, holding on to handrail. g. Jumps up and down on two feet. h. Pedals tricycle.

Infant (0-18 months) Assessment

Task: Expressing Feelings with Parents, Teachers, and Friends

	0-6 months	6-12 months	12-18 months
E1	a. Begins to self-regulate; calms self after sensitive response from a caring adult.	b. Expects adults to respond to social cues such as vocalization, gestures, or cries	c. Knows which behaviors will make caregivers react in certain ways (e.g., which actions will make you laugh and which ones will make you say "stop").
E2	a. Develops an interest in the world; is alert to sounds, touch, and faces.	b. Explores the environment; picks up objects of interest, then moves on to other objects.	c. Plays in a focused, organized manner.
E3	a. Gazes at faces with interest; smiles responsively.	b. Reaches up to indicate an interest in being held; is interested in social interaction with familiar adults.	c. Uses physical behavior (such as crawling over and pulling up) to establish closeness to caregivers.
E4	a. Seeks interactions with familiar people; vocalizes in response to vocalization.	b. Seeks to explore interesting toys, objects, and people.	c. Responds to limits that are set verbally; complies only with support from adults.
E5	a. Emotional reactions continue for a minute or two after an adult responds; does not recognize the change in state immediately.	b. Begins to coordinate behavior and emotions by acting on feelings; connects physical actions with needs (e.g., goes over to the refrigerator to indicate interest in food or drink).	c. Recovers from emotional outbursts in a few minutes most of the time.

Toddler (18-36 months) Assessment

Task: Expressing Feelings with Parents, Teachers, and Friends

	18-24 months		24-30 months	30-36 months	
E1	a. Begins to create mental images of emotional behaviors.	b. Uses behavior to express emotions (e.g., stomps foot).	c. Distinguishes between emotions and the behaviors that go with that emotion (e.g., feeling mad vs. acting mad).	d. Understands how one feeling relates to another (e.g., being disappointed about getting a toy and getting angry as a result of the disappointment).	
E2	a. Emotional intensity is not regulated—minor and major events get similar reactions; falls apart easily.		b. Begins to regulate emotional intensity in some situations; falls apart less frequently.	c. Regulates emotional intensity most of the time; seldom falls apart.	d. Figures out how to respond with appropriate emotions to most situations.
E3	a. Watches and remembers emotional behaviors exhibited by others; uses observations in future interactions.		b. Puts emotional mental images to work in pretend play; can make-believe or pretend to be angry, happy, sad, etc.		
E4	a. Knows rules that have been reinforced consistently but still needs reminders and physical adult support to comply.		b. Follows rules that have been reinforced consistently with verbal reminders and physical adult support.	c. Follows rules that have been reinforced consistently with just verbal reminders.	
E5	a. Unable to label own feelings.		b. Can label some feelings; uses the same feeling to represent many feelings (e.g., mad for angry, frustrated, irritated, unhappy, etc.).	c. Labels most of his or her own feelings; can differentiate between similar emotions and label them appropriately.	
E6	a. Unable to understand how others feel.		b. Begins to understand how others feel when observing others but not when he or she is a part of the interaction.	c. Understands how others feel when the behavior exhibited is consistent with the emotion being felt (e.g., angry child is yelling, stomping foot, saying, "No!").	
E7	a. Has difficulty delaying gratification.		b. Can delay gratification for a short time when supported by adults.	c. Can delay gratification for a few minutes in most situations.	
E8	a. Does not separate fantasy from reality.		b. Can switch from reality to fantasy.	c. Understands "real" and "not real."	
E9	a. Ambivalent about being autonomous; wants to sometimes and doesn't want to at other times.		b. Independent behaviors are increasing; dependent behaviors are decreasing.	c. Independent behaviors are usually present.	
E10	a. Has little control over impulses.		b. Controls impulses in some situations or with support from adults.	c. Most impulses are under control.	
E11	a. Loses emotional control often and intensely.		b. Loss of emotional control is less frequent, less intense, and less prolonged.	c. Infrequently loses emotional control.	

Infant (0-18 months) Observation and Assessment Summary

	0-6 months		6-12 months		12-18 months	
	Subtask	Date	Subtask	Date	Subtask	Date
Task 1 **Separating from** **Parents**	S1a		S1b		S1d	
			S1c			
	S2a		S2b		S2c	
	S3a		S3b		S3d	
			S3c			
	S4a		S4b		S4c	
	S5a		S5b		S5c	
	S6a		S6b		S6c	
	S7a		S7b		S7c	
Task 2 **Connecting with** **School and Teacher**	C1a		C1b		C1c	
	C2a		C2b		C2c	
	C3a		C3b		C3c	
	C4a		C4b		C4c	
	C5a		C5b		C5c	
	C6a		C6c		C6d	
	C6b					
	C7a		C7c		C7d	
	C7b					
	C8a		C8c		C8d	
	C8b					
Task 3 **Relating to Self and** **Others**	R1a		R1b		R1c	
	R2a		R2b		R2d	
			R2c			
	R3a		R3b		R3c	
	R4a		R4b		R4c	
	R5a		R5b		R5c	
			R5c			
	R6a		R6a		R6b	
	R7a		R7b		R7d	
			R7c			
	R8a		R8b		R8d	
			R8c			
	R9a		R9a		R9b	
	R10a		R10b		R10d	
			R10c			
	R11a		R11a		R11b	

	0-6 months		6-12 months		12-18 months	
	Subtask	Date	Subtask	Date	Subtask	Date
Task 4 **Communicating** **with Parents,** **Teachers, and Friends**	CM1a		CM1d		CM1e	
	CM1b					
	CM1c					
	CM2a		CM2c		CM2e	
	CM2b		CM2d			
	CM3a		CM3c		CM3d	
	CM3b					
	CM4a		CM4b		CM4b	
	CM5a		CM5c		CM5d	
	CM5b					
	CM6a		CM6b		CM6c	
	CM6b					
	CM7a		CM7b		CM7c	
	CM7b				CM7d	
Task 5 **Moving around** **Home and School**	M1a		M1f		M1k	
	M1b		M1g		M1l	
	M1c		M1h		M1m	
	M1d		M1i		M1n	
	M1e		M1j		M1o	
					M1p	
	M2a		M2e		M2i	
	M2b		M2f		M2j	
	M2c		M2g		M2k	
	M2d		M2h			
Task 6 **Expressing Feelings** **with Parents,** **Teachers, and Friends**	E1a		E1b		E1c	
	E2a		E2b		E2c	
	E3a		E3b		E3c	
	E4a		E4b		E4c	
	E5a		E5b		E5c	

Toddler (18-36 months) Observation and Assessment Summary

	18-24 months		24-30 months		30-36 months	
	Subtask	Date	Subtask	Date	Subtask	Date
Task 1 **Transitioning to School**	T1a		T1b		T1c	
	T2a		T2b		T2c	
	T3a		T3b		T3c	
	T4a		T4b		T4c	
	T5a		T5b		T5c	
	T6a		T6b		T6d	
			T6c			
	T7a		T7b		T7c	
Task 2 **Making Friends**	MF1a		MF1a		MF1c	
	MF2a		MF2b		MF2c	
	MF3a		MF3b		MF3c	
	MF4a		MF4b		MF4c	
	MF5a		MF5b		MF5c	
	MF6a		MF6b		MF6b	
	MF7a		MF7b		MF7c	
	MF8a		MF8b		MF8c	
	MF9a		MF9b		MF9d	
			MF9c			
	MF10a		MF10b		MF10b	
	MF11a		MF11b		MF11b	
Task 3 **Exploring Roles**	ER1a		ER1b		ER1c	
	ER2a		ER2b		ER2c	
	ER3a		ER3b		ER3c	
	ER4a		ER4b		ER4c	
Task 4 **Communicating with Parents, Teachers, and Friends**	CM1a		CM1b		CM1c	
	CM2a		CM2b		CM2c	
	CM3a		CM3b		CM3b	
	CM4a		CM4b		CM4b	
	CM5a		CM5c		CM5d	
	CM5b					
	CM6a		CM6b		CM6c	

	18-24 months		24-30 months		30-36 months	
	Subtask	Date	Subtask	Date	Subtask	Date
Task 5 **Problem-solving**	PS1a		PS1b		PS1c	
	PS2a		PS2b		PS2c	
	PS3a		PS3b		PS3c	
	PS4a		PS4d		PS4f	
	PS4b		PS4e		PS4g	
	PS4c				PS4h	
	PS5a		PS5c		PS5f	
	PS5b		PS5d		PS5g	
			PS5e		PS5h	
Task 6 **Expressing Feelings** **with Parents,** **Teachers, and Friends**	E1a		E1c		E1d	
	E1b					
	E2a		E2b		E2c	
					E2d	
	E3a		E3b		E3b	
	E4a		E4b		E4c	
	E5a		E5b		E5c	
	E6a		E6b		E6c	
	E7a		E7b		E7c	
	E8a		E8b		E8c	
	E9a		E9b		E9c	
	E10a		E10b		E10c	
	E11a		E11b		E11c	

Innovations

Completed Combined Infant and Toddler Observation/Assessment Birth-3 years

Completed Developmental Assessment

Infant (0-18 months) Assessment

Task: Separating from Parents

	0-6 months 7/13/98 – 1/13/99	6-12 months 1/13/99 – 7/13/99		12-18 months 7/13/99 – 1/13/00
S1	a. Little or no experience with separating from Mom and Dad; accepts sensitive care from substitute. 8/30/98: takes bottle from teacher	b. Some experience with separating from Mom and Dad; prefers familiar caregiver, but accepts sensitive care from substitute. See AN 10/1/98	c. More experience with separating from Mom and Dad; resists separating; shows distress upon separation, and takes time to adjust. 4/1/99	d. Experienced with separating from Mom and Dad; resists initial separation, but adjusts after only a few moments. AN: 8/16/99
S2	a. Startled by new sounds, smells, and people. 9/2/98: Door slams, Abby's cry	b. Orients toward new or interesting stimuli. 9/15/98: B&W mobile over changing table		c. Seeks new and interesting stimuli. 6/30/99
S3	a. Accepts transitions without notice. 8/13/98: Accepted transition from mom to teacher	b. Reacts with discomfort during the transition. N/O	c. Resists transition preparation as well as the transition. N/O	d. Anticipates transitions when preparation activities begin. If preparation is to a preferred, familiar activity, transition is accepted. 11/15/99
S4	a. Displays indiscriminate attachment; will accept sensitive care from most familiar adults; exhibits preference for Mom, Dad, or familiar caregiver if present. 8/30/98	b. Displays discriminate attachment; will still accept care from sensitive caregivers, but prefers care from Mom, Dad, or familiar caregivers. 3/1/99 Likes Gwynethia when Louisa at lunch		c. Separation anxiety emerges; resists approaches by unfamiliar adults and resists separation from Mom, Dad, and familiar caregivers. Cries, clings, calls for parents when they leave the child's view. 7/15/99 See com. sheet 7/15/99
S5	a. Unpredictable daily schedule. 8/30/98 See Daily Schedule Form, child file	b. Patterns in daily schedule emerge around eating and sleeping. See AN 11/30/98 See Daily Schedule Form		c. Daily schedule is predictable. Eating and sleeping patterns are relatively stable and predictable. 9/1/99
S6	a. Feeds from breast or bottle. breast milk in bottle 8/30/98	b. Begins to take baby food from a spoon; begins to sip from a cup. spoon 3/15/99 cup 7/5/99		c. Drinks from bottle and/or cup; eats finger foods. Cup only 10/10/99 finger foods 7/15/99 (AN)
S7	a. Plays with objects within visual field; bats at objects with hands and feet. 10/23/98	b. Manipulates, mouths, and plays with objects; likes action/reaction toys. Plays with objects then drops them to move on to new objects. May return to objects again and again. 2/14/99		c. Plays with favorite things again and again. Likes to dump out objects and play with them on the floor. Considers all objects and toys in the environment personal play choices, even when being played with by others. 10/30/99

Toddler (18-36 months) Assessment

Task: Transitioning to School

	18-24 months 1/13/00 – 7/13/00	**24-30 months** 7/13/00 – 1/13/01		**30-36 months** 1/13/01 – 7/13/01
T1	a. Experienced in separating from Mom and Dad; may resist initial separation in new or unusual settings, but adjusts after a few moments. *AN 11/21/99*	b. Experienced with separating; looks forward to favorite activities. May approach new or unusual settings with caution, but gets interested after a few minutes. *7/1/00*		c. Separates easily in most situations. If cautious, gets over caution quickly when invited to join in by a friendly adult or peer. *3/13/01*
T2	a. Actively seeks new and interesting stimuli; interested in everything in the environment. *2/11/00 Likes Legos*	b. May get into difficulty seeking and exploring interesting stimuli (e.g., climbing on furniture, opening off-limits cabinets). *8/19/00 Likes to climb on tables*		c. Seeks novel and interesting stimuli; when presented with familiar and novel stimuli, prefers novel ones. *AN 6/1/01 Made clean mud and played in it*
T3	a. Resists separations and transitions to unfamiliar or new settings or to settings that are not preferred. *N/O*	b. Transitions to familiar people in familiar settings easily; still cautious about unfamiliar settings or new experiences. *7/1/00*		c. Transitions to most settings without distress; when distress occurs, can be comforted or redirected. *1/1/01 Recovers in less than 5 minutes*
T4	a. Separation anxiety begins to resolve; is able to make transitions to familiar settings with familiar adults without experiencing distress. When distress occurs, it resolves when the child gets interested in the new setting and playmates. *1/27/00*	b. Stranger anxiety emerges. Fear of strangers and new situations causes proximity-seeking behavior such as getting close to primary caregiver, clinging, crying, resistance of social overtures (e.g., hiding behind adult, hiding face). *9/19/00*		c. Stranger anxiety begins resolving; may continue to be cautious, but will accept interactions from strangers after watching or observing for a moment. Takes cues (looks to them, watches their reactions) about new situations from familiar adults. *1/13/01*
T5	a. Prefers predictable routines and schedule; manages changes in schedule fairly well at the time but may experience problems later. *4/15/00 Doe better with several reminders*	b. Ritualistic about routines and schedule—likes routines predictably "just so"; exhibits ritualistic behavior around routines; likes routines the same way every time; needs warnings of anticipated transitions and still may resist them; melts down or tantrums when schedule is changed without reminders and preparation. *AN 8/16/00*		c. Adapts to changes in schedule when prepared in advance; abrupt or unplanned schedule changes still present problems; adapts more readily in familiar settings except when tired, hungry, or ill. *7/1/01*
T6	a. Tries new food when presented; has strong food preferences. *Likes pizza, p&j, crackers, apples, grapes, gr. beans, doesn't like bananas, corn, orange juice, pepperoni on pizza* *1/12/00*	b. Resists new foods on some days and not on others; reduces intake; may become a picky eater or refuse to try new foods when offered. *4/30/00*	c. Has small selection of food preferences; still resists new food when presented; eats well on some days and not on others. *10/16/00*	d. Food intake and preferences even out; will try new food after many presentations; needs encouragement to try new foods. *Tried applesauce at snack; liked it this time* *7/1/01*
T7	a. Develops a sense of property rights; hoards toys and favorite objects. *10/30/99*	b. Considers objects being played with as personal property. *6/15/00*		c. Recognizes mine and not mine. *12/17/00*

Infant (0-18 months) Assessment

Task: Connecting with School and Teacher

	0-6 months 7/13/98 – 1/13/99		6-12 months 1/13/99 – 7/13/99	12-18 months 7/13/99 – 1/13/00
C1	a. Does not resist separating from parents. 8/31/98		b. Resists separating from parents; resists comfort from primary teacher. 4/1/99	c. Resists separating from parents; accepts comfort from primary teacher. AN 8/16/99
C2	a. Accepts transition from parent to teacher. N/O		b. Maintains physical proximity to primary teacher during separation. 4/1/99	c. Seeks primary teacher's support in separating. AN 8/16/99
C3	a. Comforts after a period of distress. AN 8/30/98		b. Comforts quickly after being picked up. AN 12/6/98	c. Comforts when needs or wants are acknowledged by caregiver. AN 8/16/99
C4	a. Is unaware of friends in classroom. 9/2/98		b. Visually notices friends in classroom. 2/15/99	c. Gets excited about seeing friends; seeks physical proximity. 11/3/99
C5	a. Uses parents and teacher physically to support exploration of the environment; explores objects placed nearby parents and teachers. AN 12/6/98		b. Uses parents and teacher visually to support exploration of the environment; manipulates objects found in environment. AN 3/28/99	c. Explores the environment independently; responds to play cues presented by adults. 5/2/99
C6	a. Focuses on face-to-face interaction. 8/30/98	b. Tracks moving object up and down and right to left. 10/1/98	c. Watches people, objects, and activities in immediate environment. 1/31/99	d. Initiates interactions with people, toys, and the environment. 6/1/99
C7	a. Objects exist only when in view. 8/30/98	b. Objects perceived as having separate existence. AN 10/1/98	c. Looks where objects were last seen after they disappear. *Looked for cup on table after it fell on floor* 1/31/99	d. Follows visual displacement of objects. *Played "Where's the Kitty?" –followed 3 displacements visually* 8/15/99
C8	a. Thinks object disappears when it moves out of view. 9/2/98	b. Looks where object was last seen after it disappears. AN 11/30/98	c. Follows object as it disappears. AN 3/28/99	d. Searches for hidden object if the disappearance was observed. *Pulled blanket off of teddy after hiding it* 8/15/99

Toddler (18-36 months) Assessment

Task: Making Friends

	18-24 months 1/13/00 – 7/13/00	24-30 months 7/13/00 – 1/13/01	30-36 months 1/13/01 – 7/13/01
MF1	a. Calms self with verbal support from adults and transitional objects. 12/17/99	b. Calms self with verbal support from adults; may look for transitional objects to help with the calm-down process after verbal support is provided. Frequency of emotional outburst begins to diminish. 4/22/00	c. Calms self with only verbal support. Use of transitional objects begins to decline except at bedtime and when recovering from intense emotional outbursts. 7/13/01
MF2	a Goes to mirror to look at self; makes faces, and shows emotions like laughing, crying, and so on. AN 2/21/00	b. Calls own name when looking at photographs or in the mirror. 8/15/00	c. Calls names of friends in photographs. 6/1/01
MF3	a. Develops preferences for types of play and types of toys. Firefighter and trucks	b. Develops play themes that are repeated again and again (such as mommy or firefighter). 8/15/00	c. Begins exploration of a wider range of play themes. Themes often come from new experiences. 6/1/01 Plans to be a truck driver, loves trucks
MF4	a. Perfects gross motor skills such as running, climbing, and riding push toys. Fine motor skills with manipulatives (simple puzzles, Duplos, and so on) are emerging. 11/13/99	b. Likes physical challenges such as running fast, jumping high, and going up and down stairs. Plays with preferred manipulatives for increasing periods of time. 6/15/00	c. Competently exhibits a wide range of physical skills. Begins to be interested in practicing skills such as throwing a ball, riding a tricycle, or completing a puzzle. 7-piece puzzle 3/21/01 10-piece puzzle 5/16/01 ball 11/99; trike 2/15/01
MF5	a. Play may be onlooker, solitary, or parallel in nature. Predominantly solitary AN 1/17/00	b. Play is predominantly parallel in nature. 6/15/00	c. Exhibits associative play with familiar play partners. 4/13/01 Alexander is often chosen
MF6	a. Exhibits symbolic play. 11/21/00	b. Practices and explores a wide variety of symbolic play themes and roles. 1/13/01 3/15/01 6/21/01 7/13/01 grocery store, shoe store, firefighter, bus driver	
MF7	a. Objects to strangers presence; clings, cries, and seeks support when strangers are around. 1/17/00	b. Objection to strangers begins to diminish; may still be wary of strangers or new situations. 6/4/00	c. Is able to venture into strange or new situations if prepared in advance and supported by adults. 7/1/01
MF8	a. Uses single words to indicate needs and wants such as "muk" for "I want milk," or "bye bye" for "Let's go bye bye." See word list	b. Uses phrases and 2- to 3-word sentences to indicate needs and wants. See phrase and sentence list in file	c. Uses 4- to 6-word sentences to indicate needs and wants. AN 2/17/00
MF9	a. Connects emotions with behaviors; uses language to express these connections. 1/17/00	b. Uses emotional ideas in play. 6/15/00	c. Elaborates on emotional ideas and understanding to play with objects. 10/4/00	d. Begins emotional thinking; begins to understand emotional cause-and-effect relationships. 7/1/01
MF10	a. Takes turns with toys and materials with adult support and facilitation. 7/1/00	b. Takes turns with toys and materials with friend, sometimes without adult support. AN 2/13/01	
MF11	a. Experiments with behavior that accomplishes a goal; may bite, pinch, poke, scratch, push, and so on while trying to make things happen. 1/12/00	b. Begins to anticipate what might happen when actions are taken; chooses to make things happen if outcomes are desirable (e.g., trade toys with a friend who will stay and play), and resists taking action if outcomes are undesirable (e.g., teacher putting markers away if child chews on the tips). AN 5/13/00 AN 8/15/00 AN 2/17/00	

Infant (0-18 months) Assessment

Task: Relating to Self and Others

	0-6 months 7/13/98 – 1/13/99	6-12 months 1/13/99 – 7/13/99		12-18 months 7/13/99 – 1/13/00
R1	a. Calms self with adult support. 8/30/98	b. Calms self with support from adults and/or transitional objects. Likes silky blanket 1/16/99		c. Calms self with transitional objects. 5/19/99
R2	a. Unaware of own image in mirror. N/O	b. Curious about own image in mirrors and photographs. N/O	c. Discovers self in mirror and photographs. AN 3/16/99	d. Differentiates own image from images of others. 10/14/00
R3	a. Begins to demonstrate preferences for different types of sensory stimuli. AN 10/1/98	b. Prefers some types of stimuli to others. 11/13/99 Loves books, action/reaction toys, push/pull toys and stuffed animals		c. Is interested in pursuing favorite stimulation activities again and again. 5/1/99 Stroller rides!
R4	a. Develops a multi-sensory interest in the world—wants to see, touch, mouth, hear, and hold objects. 9/2/98	b. Uses senses to explore and discover the near environment. 3/28/99		c. Uses motor movements to enhance sensory exploration of the environment. 4/28/99
R5	a. Play is predominantly unoccupied in nature. 9/2/98	b. Play is predominantly onlooker in nature. 1/30/99	c. Play is predominantly solitary in nature. 6/1/99	
R6	a. Exhibits practice play. AN 3/16/99	AN 8/16/99		AN 11/21/00 b. Exhibits symbolic play. Likes to play firefighter
R7	a. Develops an interest in the human world. Gazes at teacher's face 9/2/98	b. Seeks interactions with responsive adults; interested also in what other children are doing. 1/31/99	c. Seeks most interactions with familiar adults; fascinated by what other children are doing. 2/14/99	d. Prefers interactions with familiar adults; resists interaction with unfamiliar adults; may be cautious with unfamiliar friends. 5/21/99
R8	a. Does not distinguish between needs (social interaction, a new position, holding instead of lying in the bed) and wants (food, diaper changes, sleep). 8/30/98	b. Begins to distinguish between needs and wants; can communicate differently about different needs and wants. 2/14/99	c. Uses objects, gestures, and behaviors to indicate needs and wants. Points and says "meomeomeo" means "milk" 2/15/99	d. Uses single words to indicate needs and wants like "muk" for "I want milk," or "bye-bye" for "Let's go bye-bye." 5/21/99 See word list
R9	a. Creates mental images of emotions and emotional responses to situations. AN 11/30/98 AN 12/6/98			b. Begins to understand how feelings relate to others. Comforted Kinsey when she cried 3/18/00
R10	a. Unable to negotiate interactions with peers without direct adult support and facilitation. 8/30/98	b. Calls for help loudly by crying or screaming when problems occur during exploration of the environment or with peers. AN 12/6/98	c. Exchanges or trades with peers to get a desired toy or material with direct adult support and facilitation. 7/14/99	d. Asks other children to walk away when conflict arises between children; expects the other child to do so. 3/1/00
R11	a. Explores environment and the things in it orally. May bite, poke, scratch, or pinch others during exploration. AN 11/30/98 AN 12/6/98 AN 8/16/99			b. Experiments with behavior that gets a reaction; may bite, pinch, poke, scratch during interactions with others to see what happens. 2/16/00

Toddler (18-36 months) Assessment

Task: Exploring Roles

	18-24 months 1/13/00 – 7/13/00	24-30 months 7/13/00 – 1/13/01	30-36 months 1/13/01 – 7/13/01
ER1	a. Explores roles related to self and family. 2/14/00	b. Explores roles related to self, friends, family, and neighborhood. AN 4/30/00	c. Explores roles related to self, friends, family, neighborhood, and the community at large. 7/13/01
ER2	a. Is unable to choose or modify behavior in response to physical or social cues of situations; persists in using behavior that doesn't work in situations. 2/14/00	b. Begins to choose or modify behavior in response to physical and social cues of situations; when one behavior isn't working, may stop and try something else. 9/15/00	c. Chooses and modifies behavior in response to the physical and social cues of a situation; tries to choose the behaviors that will get what he or she wants; can change behaviors if they are not working. 5/21/01
ER3	a. Does not understand the impact of own behavior on others. Runs into Ling Li, looks at her, keeps running 1/13/00	b. Begins to understand the impact of own behavior on others; shows interest and awareness of the emotional behaviors of friends and others. 4/30/00 Asks Maxwell why he is crying	c. Understands the impact of own behavior on others; anticipates how friends or others will react. 7/13/01
ER4	a. Uses props to play roles; becomes the occupant of the role (is superman when wearing a cape or mommy when holding a baby). Prefers familiar roles. Firefighter, see AN 11/21/00	b. Uses props to adopt roles; abandons roles when the props are removed; changes between familiar and favorite roles in dramatic play. 11/16/00	c. Can play roles with or without props. Transitions between roles frequently and easily (e.g., can be the mommy, then the daddy, then the monster during same play period). 4/13/01

Infant (0-18 months) Assessment

Task: *Communicating with Parents, Teachers, and Friends*

	0-6 months 7/13/98 – 1/13/99			6-12 months 1/13/99 – 7/13/99		12-18 months 7/13/99 – 1/13/00	
CM1	a. Gazes at familiar faces. 8/30/98	b. Responds to facial expressions of familiar faces. 8/30/98	c. Occasionally engages in reciprocal communication with facial expressions, vowel sounds, and voice inflection. 10/31/98	d. Frequently engages in reciprocal communication using facial expressions, inflection, and vowel and consonant sounds. 11/15/98		e. Imitates and jabbers in response to familiar voices. 2/15/99	
CM2	a. Makes sounds. 8/30/98	b. Imitiates intonational and inflectional vocal patterns. 11/30/98		c. Develops holophrasic speech—words that convey complete sentences or thoughts. 12/15/98	d. Uses the same word to convey different meaning. meomeomeo means milk, juice, water 1/4/99	e. Develops telegraphic speech, where 2 or 3 words are used as a sentence. 5/19/99	
CM3	a. Listens to familiar people's voices when they talk. 9/2/98	b. Shows understanding of simple phrases by responding or reacting. 12/15/98		c. Points or looks at familiar objects when asked to do so. 2/14/99		d. Follows commands with visual cues or context cues. Goes to door when teacher says it's time to go outside 5/1/99	
CM4	a. Babbles motorically, acoustically, and visually simple sounds like (m), (p), (b), (n) at the beginning of words and vowel sounds like (ah), (oh), (uh).			b. Babbles sounds like (w), (k), (f), (t), (d) at the beginning of words and vowels sounds like (eh), (ee); strings sounds together (ba-ba-ba-ba-ba) and practices sounds in a wide variety of ways. See sound list in file			
CM5	a. Responds discriminantly to voices of mother and father. 8/31/98	b. Turns toward and responds to familiar voices and sounds. 1/13/99		c. Prefers familiar sounds and voices. 2/15/99		d. Directs vocalizations toward familiar people and objects in the environment. 4/1/99	
CM6	a. Experiments with babbling and cooing. 2/15/99	b. Inflection is added to babbling and cooing. AN 3/1/99				c. Single words or phrases are understandable to familiar adults; strangers may not understand these words. See word list in file	
CM7	a. Looks at picture books. 1/30/99	b. Listens to books when read by a familiar adult. 2/14/99				c. Points to pictures. 2/14/99	d. Turns pages. 5/14/99

Toddler (18-36 months) Assessment

Task: Communicating with Parents, Teachers, and Friends

	18-24 months 1/13/00 – 7/13/00		24-30 months 7/13/00 – 1/13/01	30-36 months 1/13/01 – 7/13/01
CM1	a. Expressive vocabulary increases; uses about 200 words on a regular basis. Expressive language continues to be telegraphic, where single words may carry expanded meaning only understood by familiar caregivers. See word, phrase list		b. Vocabulary size begins to grow rapidly; sentence length begins to increase with 3 or 4 words in some sentences. See sentence list	c. Sentence length continues to grow. Four- to six-word sentences predominate expressive language. Vocabulary continues to expand; expressive vocabulary is adequate to make most needs and wants understood by others. 5/13/01
CM2	a. Uses a greater variety of sounds and sound combinations, simplifying the word if it is too complex (such as pane for plane, tephone for telephone); enjoys experimenting with inflection that sounds like adult speech although it is not yet understandable. Can understand 2/14/00 most language		b. Rapid development of new sound combinations and new words that are understandable to adults. Uses language functionally—to ask for things and get needs met and to interact with friends. 5/13/00	c. Is able to use language to get most needs and wants met by familiar caregivers and to interact with friends. 5/13/01
CM3	a. Seeks vocal interactions with familiar people; can communicate needs and wants to familiar caregivers; begins to be wary of talking to strangers. 1/11/00		b. Resists interactions with strangers; hides, withdraws, or objects to encouragement to talk to strangers. 6/4/00	
CM4	a. 20-25% of language is intelligible to strangers. Parents and caregivers can understand more. 2/14/00		b. 60-65% of language is intelligible to strangers. Parents and caregivers understand most of the child's expressive language. 2/14/00	
CM5	a. "Reads" book from front to back; turns books right side up to look at them. 2/14/00	b. Makes sounds that connect to pictures in books. 2/14/00	c. Listens to a complete story from beginning to end; asks to read familiar books over and over again. See Books Read list 2/14/00	d. Likes to look at books independently; "reads" books to self. See Books Read list 5/13/01
CM6	a. Actively experiments with the environment; follows visual displacement of objects. 8/15/99		b. Begins transition to symbolic thought. Uses formed mental images to solve problems. Thought processes relate to concrete experiences and objects. AN 6/21/00	c. Begins transition to pre-operational stage characterized by the beginning of symbolic thought and the use of mental images and words.

Task: Moving Around Home and School

0-6 months (7/13/98 - 1/13/99)

	M1	Date	M2	Date
a.	Holds head away from shoulder.	8/30/98	Eyes and head follow motion.	8/30/98
b.	Holds head steady side to side.	8/30/98	Holds rattle.	10/1/98
c.	Holds head up when lying on stomach.	9/5/98	Exchanges objects between hands.	12/23/98
d.	Rolls from back to front.	11/1/98	Uses pincher grasp to pick up small items.	1/29/99
e.	Rolls from front to back.	11/19/98	Picks up toys and objects.	12/23/98

6-12 months (1/13/99 - 7/13/99)

	M1	Date	M2	Date
f.	Scoots on stomach.	2/15/99	Dumps objects out of containers.	4/1/99
g.	Sits with support.	4/1/99	Puts objects back into containers.	5/1/99
h.	Sits without support.	5/1/99	Scribbles.	8/4/99
i.	Crawls after ball or toy.	6/1/99	—	
j.	Pulls to a stand.	6/1/99	—	

12-18 months (7/13/99 - 1/13/00)

	M1	Date	M2	Date
k.	Lowers back down to squatting position.	6/1/99	Completes puzzles with 2-3 pieces.	2/4/00
l.	Walks with support.	8/2/99	—	
m.	Walks without support.	10/1/99	—	
n.	Squats down and stands back up.	11/15/99	—	
o.	Climbs into chair.	10/1/99 11/13/99	—	
p.	Kicks ball.		—	

Additional M2 (12-18 months):
- i. Turns pages in cardboard book. — 5/4/99
- j. Unbuttons large buttons. — 12/17/99

Toddler (18-36 months) Assessment

Task: Problem-solving

	18-24 months (1/13/00 – 7/13/00)	24-30 months (7/13/00 – 1/13/01)	30-36 months (1/13/01 – 7/13/01)
PS1	a. Interest in toileting is limited to watching; may show interest in flushing toilet, sitting on the toilet, or washing hands. Interest may wax and wane quickly. 2/14/00	b. Toilet play stage of toileting; interested in playing at toileting activities such as taking off diaper, sitting on the toilet, using toilet paper, flushing the toilet, and washing hands. 10/4/00	c. Toilet practice begins; likes to repeat toileting activities again and again, with or without success. dry after nap 1/28/01 controls urine 6/15/01
PS2	a. Activity level increases; requests and seeks out motor activities. Does not control activity level without adult support; yet resists adult support in modulating activity level. 11/13/99	b. Activity level continues to increase; continues to seek out motor activities. Begins to modulate activity levels with verbal and physical adult support (i.e., slow down, take a deep breath). 4/21/00	c. Alternates between high levels of activity and periods of calm, quieter activity. Can modulate activity level with verbal reminders from adults. AN 3/31/01
PS3	a. On-task behavior begins to increase. Dramatic play 17 min. as firefighter w/Sal 2/18/00	b. Able to sustain favorite activities for increasingly longer periods of time; extends on-task play time at favorite activities to 10 minutes. Still loses interest in other activities quickly. 2/18/00	c. Stays on task at favorite manipulative activities for sustained periods of time; extends on-task play time at favorite activities to 20 minutes. Still loses interest in other activities quickly. 10/1/01
PS4	a. Carries toys around from place to place. 1/13/00 — b. Undresses; takes off shoes, socks, and clothes. 2/14/00 — c. Turns door knob to open door. 2/14/00	d. Holds cup with one hand to drink. 9/10/00 — e. Shows preference for one hand. right 10/4/00	f. Unzips zipper. 1/28/01 — g. Pulls pants up. 1/28/01 — h. Zips zipper. 1/28/01
PS5	a. Propels riding toys with feet. 5/30/00 — b. Runs; collapses to stop forward movement. 4/16/00 — c. Goes up stairs without alternating feet, holding on to handrail. N/O	d. Runs; begins to control starting and stopping. 9/10/00 — e. Balances on one foot. 9/10/00	f. Goes up stairs alternating feet, holding on to handrail. N/O — g. Jumps up and down on two feet. 6/15/01 — h. Pedals tricycle. 6/15/01

Infant (0-18 months) Assessment

Task: Expressing Feelings with Parents, Teachers, and Friends

	0-6 months 7/13/98 – 1/13/99	**6-12 months** 1/13/99 – 7/13/99	**12-18 months** 7/13/99 – 1/13/00
E1	a. Begins to self-regulate; calms self after sensitive response from a caring adult. 8/30/98	b. Expects adults to respond to social cues such as vocalization, gestures, or cries AN 3/2/99	c. Knows which behaviors will make caregivers react in certain ways (e.g., which actions will make you laugh and which ones will make you say "stop"). 9/21/00
E2	a. Develops an interest in the world; is alert to sounds, touch, and faces. 9/2/98	b. Explores the environment; picks up objects of interest, then moves on to other objects. 4/1/99	c. Plays in a focused, organized manner. 3/16/00
E3	a. Gazes at faces with interest; smiles responsively. 8/30/98	b. Reaches up to indicate an interest in being held; is interested in social interaction with familiar adults. AN 3/2/99	c. Uses physical behavior (such as crawling over and pulling up) to establish closeness to caregivers. 7/15/99
E4	a. Seeks interactions with familiar people; vocalizes in response to vocalization. 9/2/98	b. Seeks to explore interesting toys, objects, and people. 1/31/99	c. Responds to limits that are set verbally; complies only with support from adults. 9/21/99
E5	a. Emotional reactions continue for a minute or two after an adult responds; does not recognize the change in state immediately. 8/30/98	b. Begins to coordinate behavior and emotions by acting on feelings; connects physical actions with needs (e.g., goes over to the refrigerator to indicate interest in food or drink). 2/15/99	c. Recovers from emotional outbursts in a few minutes most of the time. 3/16/00

Toddler (18-36 months) Assessment

Task: Expressing Feelings with Parents, Teachers, and Friends

	18-24 months 1/13/00 – 7/13/00		24-30 months 7/13/00 – 1/13/01	30-36 months 1/13/01 – 7/13/01	
E1	a. Begins to create mental images of emotional behaviors. 12/1/99	b. Uses behavior to express emotions (e.g., stomps foot). 11/21/00	c. Distinguishes between emotions and the behaviors that go with that emotion (e.g., feeling mad vs. acting mad). 2/15/01	d. Understands how one feeling relates to another (e.g., being disappointed about getting a toy and getting angry as a result of the disappointment). 6/30/01	
E2	a. Emotional intensity is not regulated—minor and major events get similar reactions; falls apart easily. 2/14/00		b. Begins to regulate emotional intensity in some situations; falls apart less frequently. 9/15/00	c. Regulates emotional intensity most of the time; seldom falls apart. 3/10/01	d. Figures out how to respond with appropriate emotions to most situations 5/21/01
E3	a. Watches and remembers emotional behaviors exhibited by others; uses observations in future interactions. AN 11/21/00		b. Puts emotional mental images to work in pretend play; can make-believe or pretend to be angry, happy, sad, etc. AN 6/15/00 AN 7/1/01		
E4	a. Knows rules that have been reinforced consistently but still needs reminders and physical adult support to comply. N/O		b. Follows rules that have been reinforced consistently with verbal reminders and physical adult support. 9/15/00	c. Follows rules that have been reinforced consistently with just verbal reminders. 4/23/01	
E5	a. Unable to label own feelings. 12/1/99		b. Can label some feelings; uses the same feeling to represent many feelings (e.g., mad for angry, frustrated, irritated, unhappy, etc.). 1/17/00	c. Labels most of his or her own feelings; can differentiate between similar emotions and label them appropriately. AN 7/1/01	
E6	a. Unable to understand how others feel. 10/15/99		b. Begins to understand how others feel when observing others but not when he or she is a part of the interaction. 1/17/00	c. Understands how others feel when the behavior exhibited is consistent with the emotion being felt (e.g., angry child is yelling, stomping foot, saying, "No!"). AN 7/1/01	
E7	a. Has difficulty delaying gratification. 12/1/99		b. Can delay gratification for a short time when supported by adults. 10/17/00	c. Can delay gratification for a few minutes in most situations. 4/23/01	
E8	a. Does not separate fantasy from reality. 12/1/99		b. Can switch from reality to fantasy. 9/15/00	c. Understands "real" and "not real." AN 7/1/01	
E9	a. Ambivalent about being autonomous; wants to sometimes and doesn't want to at other times. 12/1/99		b. Independent behaviors are increasing; dependent behaviors are decreasing. 6/15/00	c. Independent behaviors are usually present. 4/23/01	
E10	a. Has little control over impulses. 10/15/99		b. Controls impulses in some situations or with support from adults. 6/15/00	c. Most impulses are under control. AN 7/1/01	
E11	a. Loses emotional control often and intensely. AN 11/21/99		b. Loss of emotional control is less frequent, less intense, and less prolonged. 6/15/00	c. Infrequently loses emotional control. AN 7/1/01	

Infant (0-18 months) Observation and Assessment Summary

	0-6 months		6-12 months		12-18 months	
	Subtask	Date	Subtask	Date	Subtask	Date
Task 1 **Separating from Parents**	S1a	8/30/98	S1b	10/1/98	S1d	8/16/99
			S1c	4/1/99		
	S2a	9/2/98	S2b	9/15/98	S2c	6/30/99
	S3a	8/13/98	S3b	N/O	S3d	11/15/99
			S3c	N/O		
	S4a	8/30/98	S4b	3/1/99	S4c	7/15/99
	S5a	8/30/98	S5b	11/30/98	S5c	9/1/99
	S6a	8/30/98	S6b	3/15/ 7/5/99	S6c	7/15 10/10/99
	S7a	10/23/98	S7b	2/14/99	S7c	10/30/99
Task 2 **Connecting with School and Teacher**	C1a	8/31/98	C1b	4/1/99	C1c	8/16/99
	C2a	N/O	C2b	4/1/99	C2c	8/16/99
	C3a	8/30/98	C3b	12/6/98	C3c	8/16/99
	C4a	9/2/98	C4b	2/15/99	C4c	11/3/99
	C5a	12/6/98	C5b	3/28/99	C5c	5/2/99
	C6a	8/30/98	C6c	1/31/99	C6d	6/1/99
	C6b	10/1/98				
	C7a	8/30/98	C7c	1/31/99	C7d	8/15/99
	C7b	10/1/98				
	C8a	9/2/98	C8c	3/28/99	C8d	8/15/99
	C8b	11/30/98				
Task 3 **Relating to Self and Others**	R1a	8/30/98	R1b	1/16/99	R1c	5/19/99
	R2a	N/O	R2b	N/O	R2d	10/14/00
			R2c	3/16/99		
	R3a	10/1/98	R3b	11/13/99	R3c	5/1/99
	R4a	9/2/98	R4b	3/28/99	R4c	4/28/99
	R5a	9/2/98	R5b	1/30/99	R5c	
			R5c	6/1/99		
	R6a	3/16/99	R6a	8/16/99	R6b	11/21/00
	R7a	9/2/98	R7b	1/31/99	R7d	5/21/99
			R7c	2/14/99		
	R8a	8/30/98	R8b	2/14/99	R8d	5/21/99
			R8c	2/15/99		
	R9a	11/30/98, 12/6/98	R9a		R9b	3/18/00
	R10a	8/30/98	R10b	12/6/98	R10d	3/1/00
			R10c	7/14/99		
	R11a	11/30/98, 12/6/98	R11a	8/16/99	R11b	2/16/00

	0-6 months		6-12 months		12-18 months	
	Subtask	Date	Subtask	Date	Subtask	Date
Task 4 **Communicating** **with Parents,** **Teachers, and Friends**	CM1a	8/30/98	CM1d	11/15/98	CM1e	2/15/99
	CM1b	8/30/98				
	CM1c	10/31/98				
	CM2a	8/30/98	CM2c	12/15/98	CM2e	5/19/99
	CM2b	11/30/98	CM2d	1/4/99		
	CM3a	9/2/98	CM3c	2/14/99	CM3d	5/1/99
	CM3b	12/15/98				
	CM4a		CM4b	See sound list	CM4b	
	CM5a	8/31/98	CM5c	2/15/99	CM5d	4/1/99
	CM5b	1/13/99				
	CM6a	2/15/99	CM6b	3/1/99	CM6c	See word list
	CM6b					
	CM7a	1/30/99	CM7b	2/14/99	CM7c	2/14/99
	CM7b				CM7d	5/14/99
Task 5 **Moving around** **Home and School**	M1a	8/30/98	M1f	2/15/99	M1k	6/1/99
	M1b	8/30/98	M1g	4/1/99	M1l	8/2/99
	M1c	9/15/98	M1h	5/1/99	M1m	10/1/99
	M1d	11/1/98	M1i	6/1/99	M1n	11/15/99
	M1e	11/19/98	M1j	6/1/99	M1o	10/1/99
					M1p	11/13/99
	M2a	8/30/98	M2e	12/23/98	M2i	5/14/99
	M2b	10/1/98	M2f	4/1/99	M2j	12/17/99
	M2c	12/23/98	M2g	5/14/99	M2k	2/14/01
	M2d	1/29/99	M2h	8/14/99		
Task 6 **Expressing Feelings** **with Parents,** **Teachers, and Friends**	E1a	8/30/98	E1b	3/2/99	E1c	9/21/00
	E2a	9/2/98	E2b	4/1/99	E2c	3/16/00
	E3a	8/30/98	E3b	3/2/99	E3c	7/15/99
	E4a	9/2/98	E4b	1/31/99	E4c	9/21/99
	E5a	8/30/98	E5b	2/15/99	E5c	3/16/00

	18-24 months		24-30 months		30-36 months	
	Subtask	Date	Subtask	Date	Subtask	Date
Task 1 **Transitioning to** **School**	T1a	11/21/99	T1b	7/1/00	T1c	3/13/01
	T2a	2/11/00	T2b	8/19/00	T2c	6/1/01
	T3a	N/O	T3b	7/1/00	T3c	1/1/01
	T4a	1/27/00	T4b	9/19/00	T4c	1/13/01
	T5a	4/15/00	T5b	8/16/00	T5c	7/1/01
	T6a	1/12/00	T6b	4/30/00	T6d	7/1/01
			T6c	10/16/00		
	T7a	10/30/99	T7b	6/15/00	T7c	12/17/00
Task 2 **Making Friends**	MF1a	12/17/99	MF1b	4/22/00	MF1c	7/13/01
	MF2a	2/21/00	MF2b	8/15/00	MF2c	6/1/01
	MF3a		MF3b	8/15/00	MF3c	6/1/01
	MF4a	11/13/99	MF4b	6/15/00	MF4c	11/1/99, 2/15/01
	MF5a	1/17/00	MF5b	6/15/00	MF5c	4/13/01
	MF6a	11/21/00	MF6b	1/13/01	MF6b	3/15/01, 6/21/01
	MF7a	1/17/00	MF7b	6/4/00	MF7c	7/1/01
	MF8a	See word list	MF8b	See file	MF8c	2/17/00
	MF9a	1/17/00	MF9b	6/15/00	MF9d	7/1/01
			MF9c	10/4/00		
	MF10a	7/1/00	MF10b		MF10b	2/13/01
	MF11a	1/17/00	MF11b	5/13/00, 8/5/00	MF11b	
Task 3 **Exploring Roles**	ER1a	2/14/00	ER1b	4/30/00	ER1c	7/13/01
	ER2a	2/14/00	ER2b	9/15/00	ER2c	5/21/01
	ER3a	1/13/00	ER3b	4/30/00	ER3c	7/13/01
	ER4a	11/21/00	ER4b	11/16/00	ER4c	4/13/01
Task 4 **Communicating with** **Parents, Teachers, and** **Friends**	CM1a	see word, phrase list	CM1b	See sentences list	CM1c	5/13/01
	CM2a	2/14/00	CM2b	5/13/00	CM2c	5/13/01
	CM3a	1/11/00	CM3b	6/4/00	CM3b	
	CM4a	2/14/00	CM4b	2/14/00	CM4b	
	CM5a	2/14/00	CM5c	2/14/00	CM5d	5/13/01
	CM5b	2/14/00				
	CM6a	8/15/99	CM6b	6/21/00	CM6c	

	18-24 months		24-30 months		30-36 months	
	Subtask	Date	Subtask	Date	Subtask	Date
Task 5 **Problem-solving**	PS1a	2/14/00	PS1b	10/4/00	PS1c	1/28/01, 6/15/01
	PS2a	11/13/99	PS2b	4/21/00	PS2c	3/31/01
	PS3a	2/18/00	PS3b	2/18/00	PS3c	10/11/01
	PS4a	1/13/00	PS4d	9/10/00	PS4f	1/28/01
	PS4b	2/14/00	PS4e	10/4/00	PS4g	1/28/01
	PS4c	2/14/00			PS4h	1/28/01
	PS5a	5/3/00	PS5c	N/O	PS5f	N/O
	PS5b	4/16/00	PS5d	9/10/00	PS5g	6/15/01
			PS5e	9/10/00	PS5h	6/15/01
Task 6 **Expressing Feelings with Parents, Teachers, and Friends**	E1a	12/1/99	E1c	2/15/01	E1d	6/30/01
	E1b	11/21/00				
	E2a	2/14/00	E2b	9/15/00	E2c	3/10/01
					E2d	5/21/01
	E3a	11/21/00	E3b	6/15/00	E3b	7/1/01
	E4a	N/O	E4b	9/15/00	E4c	4/23/01
	E5a	12/1/99	E5b	1/17/00	E5c	7/1/01
	E6a	10/15/99	E6b	1/17/00	E6c	7/1/01
	E7a	12/1/99	E7b	10/17/00	E7c	4/23/01
	E8a	12/1/99	E8b	9/15/00	E8c	7/1/01
	E9a	12/1/99	E9b	6/15/00	E9c	4/23/01
	E10a	10/15/99	E10b	6/15/00	E10c	7/1/01
	E11a	11/21/99	E11b	6/15/00	E11c	7/1/01

Index

Y

Young Children, 159

Z

Zone of proximal development, 146

Innovations

Kay Albrecht and Linda G. Miller

Everything you need for a complete infant and toddler program. The *Innovations* curriculum series is a comprehensive, interactive curriculum for infants and toddlers. Responding to children's interests is at the heart of emergent curriculum and central to the *Innovations* series, which meets the full spectrum of needs for teachers, parents, and the children they care for. In addition to the wealth of activities, each book includes these critical components:

- Applying child development theory to everyday experiences
- Using assessment to meet individual developmental needs of infants and toddlers
- Using the physical environment as a learning tool
- Developing a partner relationship with parents
- Fostering an interactive climate in the classroom
- Educating parents

The *Innovations* series is a unique combination of the practical and theoretical. It combines them in a way that provides support for beginning teachers, information for experienced teachers, and a complete program for every teacher!

Innovations: The Comprehensive Infant Curriculum

416 pages

ISBN 0-87659-213-2 / Gryphon House / 14962 / $39.95

Innovations: The Comprehensive Toddler Curriculum

416 pages

ISBN 0-87659-214-0 / Gryphon House / 17846 / $39.95

Available at your favorite bookstore, school supply store, or order directly from
Gryphon House at 800.638.0928 or www.gryphonhouse.com

Self-Directed Teachers' Guides to
THE
Innovations
CURRICULUM

A comprehensive (40+ hour) self-paced instructional guide is just what teachers need to effectively implement one of the best infant and toddler curriculum resources, *Innovations*: *The Comprehensive Infant Curriculum* and *Innovations: The Comprehensive Toddler Curriculum*. 128 pages each.

Innovations: The Comprehensive Infant Curriculum
A Self-Directed Teacher's Guide

Linda G. Miller and Kay Albrecht

ISBN 0-87659-270-1 / Gryphon House / 15384 / PB $12.95

Innovations: The Comprehensive Toddler Curriculum
A Self-Directed Teacher's Guide

Linda G. Miller and Kay Albrecht

ISBN 0-87659-233-7 / Gryphon House / 16571 / PB $12.95

Innovations: Infant & Toddler Development

Kay Albrecht and Linda G. Miller

Understanding infant and toddler behavior can be a challenge. But this **Innovations** book provides teachers with a more thorough understanding of the knowledge base that informs early childhood practice. Focusing on the development of children from birth to age three, **Innovations: Infant and Toddler Development** provides an in-depth discussion of the underlying ages and stages, theories, and best practices of the early childhood field. This enables teachers to begin to address these challenging behaviors in developmentally appropriate ways. 372 pages.

ISBN 0-87659-259-0 / Gryphon House / 19237 / PB / $39.95

Games to Play with Babies-3rd Edition

Jackie Silberg

Hundreds of games to play with your baby to encourage bonding, coordination, motor skills, and more!

At last...the eagerly awaited new edition of one of the most trusted and popular books on infant development is here! Completely redesigned, with 50 brand-new games and all new illustrations, this indispensable book shows you how to build important developmental skills while enjoying time with your baby. Use these everyday activities to nurture and stimulate self-confidence, coordination, social skills, and much, much more. Give your baby a great start with this wonderful collection of over 225 fun-filled games! 256 pages.

ISBN 0-87659-162-4 / Gryphon House / 16285 / PB / $14.95

Available at your favorite bookstore, school supply store, or order directly from
Gryphon House at 800.638.0928 or www.gryphonhouse.com

Early Learning Environments That Work

Rebecca Isbell and Betty Exelby

The classroom environment is a vital part of a child's learning experience. ***Early Learning Environments That Work*** explores how you can work with furniture, color, materials, storage, lighting, and more to encourage learning through classroom arrangement. Each chapter gives you detailed illustrations and photographs to help you set up or arrange what you already have in the classroom. 192 pages.

ISBN 0-87659-256-6 / Gryphon House / 14387 / PB $24.95

Early Childhood Workshops That Work!

The Essential Guide to Successful Workshops and Training

Nancy P. Alexander

This comprehensive guide illustrates how to design, organize, conduct, and evaluate effective workshop and training seminars. It also includes sections on troubleshooting and designing learning materials. ***Early Childhood Workshops That Work!*** shows you how to make your training effective, interactive, and rewarding! 192 pages.

ISBN 0-87659-215-9 / Gryphon House / 13876 / PB $29.95

Available at your favorite bookstore, school supply store, or order directly from
Gryphon House at 800.638.0928 or www.gryphonhouse.com

Notes